Chicago Public Library
Mabel Manning Branch
6 South Hoyne 60612

THE PRAIRIE GIRL'S GUIDE TO LIFE

JENNIFER WORICK

THE PRAIRIE GIRL'S GUIDE TO LIFE

How to Sew a Sampler Quilt & 49 Other Pioneer Projects for the Modern Girl

The Taunton Press

Text © 2007 by Jennifer Worick

Illustrations © 2007 by Michael Halbert

All rights reserved.

The Taunton Press, Inc.
63 South Main Street, PO Box 5506
Newtown, CT 06470-5506
e-mail: tp@taunton.com

Editor: Katie Benoit
Copy editor: Diane Sinitsky
Interior design: Chika Azuma
Illustrator: Michael Halbert

Library of Congress Cataloging-in-Publication Data
Worick, Jennifer.
The prairie girl's guide to life / author, Jennifer Worick.
p. cm.
Includes index.
ISBN 978-1-56158-986-9
1. Handicraft. 2. Cookery. I. Title.

TT157.W6385 2007
745.5--dc22

2007008998

Printed in the United States of America
10 9 8 7 6 5 4 3 2

The following manufacturers appearing in *The Prairie Girl's Guide to Life* are registered trademarks: Avery®; Ball® jar; Barbie®; Bisquick®; BlackBerry®; Clinique®; Crate and Barrel®; DMC®; Endust®; French's® French Fried Onions; Hot Wheels®; Jean Naté®; JELL-O®; John Deere™; Johnson's® Baby Shampoo; Lipton®; Microsoft® Word; Minwax® Wood Finish™; Murphy® Oil Soap; Music Together®; Noxzema®; PAM®; Polartec®; Pottery Barn®; Rolodex®; Rust-Oleum®; Sidekick®; Ultrasuede®; VistaPrint®

R0420757029

Chicago Public Library
Mabel Manning Branch
6 South Hoyne 60612

Dedication

For the many Woricks, Hamlins,
Steinbachers, and Miltzes
who came before me, true pioneers all

Acknowledgments

This book has been a long and loving time in the making. I wish I could say it was as easy as (rhubarb) pie to write all by myself, but it took a team of publishing professionals, friends, family, and kind strangers to help me craft this prairie girl's guide to skills both practical and whimsical.

First, I have to thank my agent, the lovely Joy Tutela of the David Black Literary Agency, for encouraging and assisting me from the get-go. Editor Katie Benoit and the rest of the team at The Taunton Press—Kathleen Williams, Michael Halbert, Diane Sinitsky, and Chika Azuma—have been a dream to work with. I'm lucky to have worked with a team who shares my passion for all things prairie.

Elizabeth Hechtman, MS, has also been with me every step of the way, helping me to grow as a writer, person, and businesswoman. In addition to the talented experts detailed on pp. 192–196, friends Sacha Adorno, Kerry Colburn, Gina Johnston, Melissa McDaniels, Benjamin Marra, Tekla Nachbar, Mary and Ron Ruggiero, Kerry Sturgill, Laurel Rivers, Jennifer Schaefer, Jared Von Arx, and Don

Walters provided guidance, encouragement, and their Rolodexes throughout the writing process. The generous folks at Cascade Yarns donated yarn for a rustic knitted shawl project. For all of this assistance, I am forever grateful.

Finally, I'd be nowhere without my family. This book is partly a love letter to our collective farming history, and I'm thankful for the experiences I've shared with them and the information they've so cheerfully shared with me. In particular, my mom Judy Eckelbarger, dad Willis Worick, stepmom Pat Worick, stepdad Jim Eckelbarger, brothers Chris and John Worick, stepsister Amy Crisenbery, and uncle Greg Hamlin stunned me with their knowledge of practical and inventive skills. It's little wonder we were so successful on the farm.

CONTENTS

THE SPIRIT OF LAURA LIVES ON

As a tomboy growing up in rural Michigan in the '70s with my two older brothers, I often had to fend for myself when it came to entertainment. Swinging from barn rafters, picking wildflowers, and creating forts out of snow or blankets had their charms, but I always returned to my favorite activity.

I read.

And as I opened *Little House in the Big Woods*, I no longer felt lonely or bored or unfortunate to live in the country. I felt *blessed*.

In the pages of the *Little House* series, I found a friend and heroine in Laura Ingalls Wilder. Her simple life, work ethic, and innocent pleasures transported me from my ranch house to her homestead. I was caught up in all the activities of the Ingallses' everyday life: Ma making a pie, Pa working the harvest, Laura studying for her teaching certificate, everyone drinking lemonade and watching the buggy races on Independence Day.

I wanted to learn all their skills. I wanted to fill my hope chest with handmade treasures and my table with home cooking. That desire has stayed with me as I've learned to knit, fish, make jewelry, bake pies, chop wood, make lip balm, and lay a fire. And I'm not alone. I continually meet women (and men) who are embroidering and canning and putting their own twists on old-school crafts and skills. Forget about granny chic; this is *prairie* chic, and it's spreading like wildfire.

There's a reason why women want to return to the prairie, to simpler times. In fact, there are many. There's the immense pleasure of seeing the fruits of your labors. Grabbing takeout has its place but is not nearly as satisfying as making a hearty beef stew or rolling out your own pie crust. With many rustic handicrafts, you are creating family heirlooms. My home is filled with quilts, rag rugs, and knitted items that my grandmothers, my friends, or I made. While I tire of certain styles and ill-advised purchases, I would never dream of tossing out the quilted pillow my pal Susie made for me, and I hope to pass on to a son or daughter the Amish throw that I spent one winter knitting.

In addition, I love knowing that I'll be able to thrive in the most rugged of environments (such as the cabin in the woods that looked much better on the rental agency's website). In researching one of my previous books, I talked to a survival expert who taught me how to start a fire, trap and eat small game, build a snow cave, signal a plane, and identify various foodstuffs in their natural environment. Discovering that lipstick and hand sanitizer could be used as fire starter and that perfume could sterilize a wound was incredibly empowering. I wanted more.

In the course of researching this book (because lord knows I didn't know how to ice fish), I discovered that we aren't so removed from our pioneer roots as one would think. And when I sent out the call to my friends and family, I received immediate responses from people who know how to make ice cream, embroider, and even whittle.

Many experts came from my family. My brother Chris told me about his passion for panning for gold in the hills of Georgia. Mom shared her bread-and-butter pickles recipe. Dad related his memories of growing up on a farm, milking cows, gathering eggs, and harvesting crops—things I had never asked him about before. Inadvertently, I discovered perhaps the best reason of all to delve into rustic skills and handicrafts: It's a wonderful way to connect with your family and its history. It's a way of bringing the past with you into the future. My family name may not be Ingalls or Wilder, but we Woricks have been farmers for hundreds of years, and the story of our family is intertwined with the history of our great pioneering country. I don't want to lose that. So

I'm asking questions, preserving faded pictures, and making rhubarb pie. I've never felt so connected to my kin and the world.

And it's got nothing to do with geography. I can live in the city, far away from my homestead, and still feel that bond. I have my memories to tie me to my family.

My family is full of collectors, and what we collect reflects not only our interests but also our history. Our ranch-style house was decorated with farm tools (Dad), collectible cone-top beer cans (brother John), military memorabilia (brother Chris), baskets (Mom), dolls and Nancy Drew Mystery stories (that would be me).

I turned away from actively collecting a while back (although I still have my *Nancy Drew* collection)—now I make things. Like any good farm stock, I can't let my hands lie idle. I knit during *American Idol* and design jewelry while watching *Project Runway*. I write long into the night. But I lack the hard physical labor that would offer me a good night's sleep. My mind races when I climb under the quilt, perhaps because I feel that I could have accomplished more that day. Perhaps my busy mind is just matching the pace of my busy hands.

It was the knitting that pulled me back. It reconnected me with not only my past but also the rich legacy of women. It's so satisfying to make something with your own two hands, and it's even more gratifying to give a handcrafted item as a gift. I feel that I am creating heirlooms. The shawls that I wrap carefully with paper and sachets are intended for my future children. Meanwhile, I enjoy the comments and compliments I receive from strangers and friends alike when I wear a hand-knitted garment. These days, I value a pink cabled cardigan that took me a year to knit more than my designer shoe collection.

I never thought I'd say that.

And I never thought I'd hear it from every woman I meet these days. There are renegade craft fairs popping up across the land. Gals are taking up sewing, enrolling in meat-curing classes, checking out quilting and yarn expos, creating shrines to Martha Stewart. They may not realize it, but each of these women is a prairie gal.

You are a prairie gal.

And as a prairie gal, you've come to the right place. *The Prairie Girl's Guide to Life* offers every crafty and able-bodied pioneer spirit a sampling of skills, crafts, and projects that were found in every room of a prairie homestead. If you already embroider, here's the opportu-

nity to try your hand at knitting or quilting before committing significant money and resources. If you know how to make jam, why not try pickles? And what woman doesn't want to find her own gold? These projects are perfect for the beginner and experienced crafter alike. After all, not every gal was fortunate enough to be born Laura Ingalls and learn from loving and inventive parents from an early age. But there's still hope, because within all of us is a curious, pioneering spirit that drives us to travel into uncharted territories. And these days, instead of unexplored lands, we venture into the world of skills and crafts.

This book is organized around the various rooms and areas of the homestead: the Kitchen, Bedroom, Bathroom, Parlor, and Barn and Beyond. Crafts and skills that relate to each room are featured in each chapter, along with a party idea that relates to the chapter. Why hide your prairie light under a bushel? Host an ice cream social or quilting bee and spread the word. After all, if Laura Ingalls Wilder is any indication, prairie gals are as social as they are resourceful.

And which one of us doesn't want to be like Laura? I, for one, have had a lovely adventure delving into my family history and learning (or relearning) rustic skills. I may not have grown up on the prairie proper, but it's my state of mind, nimble fingers, and moxie that make me a prairie girl. And in the following pages, you'll discover more than a few projects to add to your own bag of prairie tricks. Perhaps you'll be inspired to sit down—along with a perfect pot of tea and thick slice of rhubarb pie—and talk for a spell with your kin. They might share some memories with you and, in return, maybe you can teach them a thing or two. Come to think of it, it sounds like just the kind of rewarding and industrious visit Laura would have enjoyed.

Doings: "fixins" for a meal.

"Since Ma was visiting a sick relative, Diana had to gather the doings for supper."

THE KITCHEN

Since I grew up on rural Michigan farmland, you'd think my experience in the kitchen would be extensive. But, rather, I'd arrive home from school only to have my mom slide a plate of slightly burnt Cowboy Cookies toward me as she ran out the door to her waitress job.

I didn't have a lot of hands-on practice on a daily basis, so I took matters into my own hands and set up a teahouse in my bedroom. Even then, I aspired to live in a more genteel time, an era where a girl learned how to bake pies and ride sidesaddle and blush when a young man looked in her direction.

I draped a pink gingham tablecloth over my tiny table, drew the ice-cream-parlor chairs to it, and turned my attention to the menu. At 10 years old, I had limited culinary skills, so I kept it simple: scrambled eggs and toast, BLTs, and various sandwich combinations made out of the lunchmeat samplers tucked in the crisper with the iceberg lettuce. I whipped up some JELL-O® and chocolate pudding for dessert options.

I opened for business, with my parents as my first—and only—clients. I whisked up scrambled eggs and added buttered toast on the side, just like any self-respecting prairie girl would serve. My parents humored me, encouraged me, and even left me a 25-cent tip!

My experience in the kitchen wasn't limited to slapping together bologna sandwiches. I helped to make pickles, can applesauce, roll out pie dough, stuff a turkey, and shuck peas, lima beans, and corn. These were special occasions, when I was able to connect with my busy working mom and my German grandma. I loved meting things out with our tin measuring spoons. I loved getting my hands into a bowl of hamburger and molding the goo into a meat loaf. I loved kneading dough, stirring up a cloud of flour as I worked it with my hands and a battered rolling pin. I felt like a real farmwoman, toiling over kitchen labors in order to reward myself and my family with a hard-won, home-cooked meal.

And to this day, I treat food as a reward for working hard. Eating isn't the only satisfaction. I am profoundly affected by the preparation, cooking, and presenting of food. Even when eating alone in my urban sprawl, I take time to set the table, light a candle, and appreciate the ritual of sitting down to dinner.

BRINE, TRUSS, AND ROAST A TURKEY

I can't think of turkey without thinking about Thanksgiving. Turkey and Thanksgiving go hand in hand because both came to my family's table only once a year. Pies were baked in advance and put in the oven to warm while we ate, and potatoes were peeled and boiled *en masse*. We also had the classic Midwestern delicacy: green bean casserole, complete with French's® French Fried Onions on top of it. Cranberry mold, dinner rolls, and corn rounded out the feast.

And, of course, there was the turkey, which we prepared in typical prairie fashion. We started the preparations early in the day, boiling the giblets. After they cooled, we diced them and threw them into the stuffing. We sautéed onions and celery in sticks of butter and, along

> Poor as Job's turkey:
> very poor.
> *"If she lost her satchel, Bess would be as poor as Job's turkey."*

WHAT YOU WILL NEED

Roasting pan

Large container for the brine

Clean, large towel

Trussing needle

Cotton twine

Meat thermometer

Basting brush

2 cups table salt

2 gallons cold water

One 18- to 22-pound turkey, preferably fresh

¼ cup butter

Cracked black pepper

IF NOT FILLING THE CAVITY WITH BREAD STUFFING, YOU'LL NEED:

Salt

Black pepper

5 cloves garlic

5 to 6 sprigs fresh thyme

10 carrots, cut in 3-inch chunks

10 stalks of celery, cut in 3-inch chunks

with liberal amounts of dried sage, mixed it together with day-old bread we had ripped into chunks. We added broth to soften everything up. I mixed the huge bowl of stuffing with my hands, then packed the turkey cavity with stuffing.

These days, I enlist the help of many friends to pull off a meal to remember. There's no green bean casserole in sight, but as long as the turkey and stuffing are plentiful, I barely miss it. I was recently introduced to the wonder of a brined turkey. Culinary whiz Elise Ballard Gilbert showed me the way to the promised land of succulent, savory turkey.

TIP ☞ *If your turkey isn't fresh, defrost it a day in advance.*

First, make sure you have an ample-size oven. Turkeys are very large birds—usually between 12 and 22 pounds—and require an oven that allows heated air to circulate at all angles of the bird. Your bird needs at least 6 inches of clearance from skin to oven wall to cook evenly. If your oven is small, consider following this recipe for a whole breast of turkey or a whole chicken.

Any roasting pan will do for roasting a turkey, so long as it is large enough to allow 1 to 2 inches of clearance between the bird and pan edge, and the bird is suspended above the bottom of the pan. If you don't have a roasting rack, improvise. Create a crosshatch of carrots and celery, but be aware that it will be trickier to flip the bird during the cooking process.

TIP *To get the bird ready for stuffing and trussing, avoid slips and messes by working on a clean, large, slightly damp towel.*

Brining the Bird

Brining involves soaking the bird in a saltwater bath. It makes for crispier skin and juicy, more flavorful meat. I was a disbeliever at first but was soon won over after my first bite.

Start by adding 1 cup of salt per gallon of cold water to a large container (2 gallons is sufficient for most birds, but more may be needed if your bird is larger than 18 pounds). The size of your turkey does not change the amount of salt used in your brine. And unless you want a really salty bird, do not brine a kosher or self-basting turkey, which already contains a significant amount of sodium.

Dunk your turkey into the brine solution, and place the container into your refrigerator. Allow the bird to soak in the brine for 4 to 6 hours, depending on its size (the bigger the bird, the longer the soaking time).

If you don't have room in your refrigerator for the brine container, use a cooler and a few bottles of frozen water. Using warm tap water instead of cold, stir the water vigorously to dissolve the salt, then add the frozen water bottles to cool the water to approximately 40°F. Dunk the turkey and close the cooler lid. The water bottles should keep the turkey at a safe temperature for the 4- to 6-hour brining window.

Remove the bird from the brine, and rinse it well under cold water, inside and out. Pat the turkey dry with paper towels.

TIP☞ *I've always enjoyed the stuffing that comes out of the bird, but if you would rather cook it separately, try stuffing the cavity loosely (after salting and peppering it thoroughly) with a handful of garlic cloves, fresh thyme, carrots, and celery.*

Trussing the Bird

The most effective way to truss—or tie up—a bird is by using a trussing needle, which you can find at kitchen shops and gourmet grocery stores. If you are going to stuff the bird, do it just before you truss the turkey. Tuck the tips of the drumsticks into the skin at the tail to secure, and tuck the wing tips behind the back. Thread cotton twine through the needle's eye, and sew up the cavity with a few stitches, looping the twine around the drumsticks if they won't stay put. That's it. Any more trussing and you run the risk of cooking your bird unevenly.

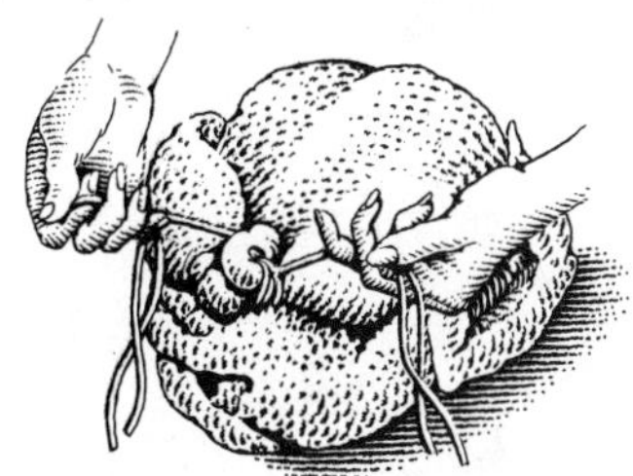

Cooking the Bird

Adjust the oven rack to the lowest position, and preheat the oven to 400°F for a 12- to 18-pound bird, 425°F for a larger turkey. Melt the butter in a saucepan, then brush the butter on the breast to cover the surface. Place the turkey breast side down on the roasting rack, and roast for 45 to 60 minutes (depending on the size of the bird). Grind a good amount of cracked black pepper over the surface of the bird.

Remove the roasting pan from the oven (close the oven door to retain heat). Reduce the temperature to 325°F. Using clean pot holders or kitchen towels, rotate the turkey breast side up, and baste the entire surface of the bird with the pan drippings. Continue to roast, basting every 20 minutes, until the thickest part of the breast registers 165°F and the thickest part of the thigh registers 170°F to 175°F on an instant-read thermometer (about 50 to 60 minutes longer for a 12- to 15-pound bird, about 1¼ hours for a 15- to 18-pound bird, or about

2 hours longer for an 18- to 22-pound bird). Legs should move freely in the joint, and when the bird is pricked, the juices should run clear.

Transfer your turkey to a carving board; let it rest for 30 to 40 minutes. Carve, serve, and tuck into your turkey.

Roasting time: 1½ to 3 hours, plus resting time of 30 to 40 minutes

CREATE THE PERFECT STEW WITH CORN BREAD

Stew seems to be one dish that men can excel at without feeling like womenfolk, perhaps because it's hearty and sticks to your bones. My dad used to whip up a decent beef stew, but what really pushed it over the edge of delicious were the Bisquick® dumplings that topped it. With a light, fluffy dumpling sopping up stew juice, what's not to like? Well, the celery, but I can forgive that.

Stew will always have a place in my heart and stomach. Pairing it with corn bread seemed like a sweet alternative to the dumpling. I'm mad for good corn bread. At a friend's jalapeño-themed party last year, I was introduced to Elise's

WHAT YOU WILL NEED

Large cast-iron skillet or Dutch oven with lid

Cheesecloth

Cooking twine

---

4 pounds beef (stew meat or a better cut), cut into 2-inch pieces

Salt, to season

Black pepper, to season

1 cup all-purpose flour

⅓ cup olive oil

2 large onions, diced

6 ounces tomato paste

1 cup red wine, the drier the better

BROTH:
1 cup beef broth
1 cup chicken broth
2 cups water

OR

4 cups freshly made beef stock (note that fresh beef stock contains less sodium, so you might need to add to the seasoning)

Salt, to taste (approximately 1 tablespoon)

Black pepper, to taste (approximately 1 tablespoon)

SPICE SATCHEL:
1 bay leaf
6 to 8 whole peppercorns
2 to 3 sprigs of various herbs such as thyme and rosemary (if using dried herbs, use 1 tablespoon dried thyme and 1 tablespoon dried rosemary and add directly to the pot)

4 cups potatoes, cut into 2-inch chunks

2 cups carrots, cut into 2-inch chunks

1 cup celery, cut into 2-inch chunks

2 cups corn, frozen or cut off the cob

1 cup peas (if frozen, thaw them before adding to the stew)

spicy corn bread. She's a true prairie girl, just the gal to teach me the basics of stew and corn-bread making.

Beef Stew

First, brown your meat. Trim the beef and season with salt and pepper, then coat the chunks in the flour. Heat a few tablespoons of the oil in a large cast-iron skillet or Dutch oven over medium-high heat until the oil shimmers and coats the bottom of the skillet easily. Brown all sides of the meat, a few pieces at a time, adding more oil as necessary. Your goal here is to brown just the outsides of the beef, without cooking all the way through. Once you've browned all the meat, transfer it to a plate.

Preheat the oven at 325°F.

> **Make a fist:**
> to succeed at something.
> *"Jessica made a poor fist when it came to cooking."*

Using the same skillet, cook the onions over medium heat until tender, about 10 minutes. Add the tomato paste, cooking for 3 minutes and scraping the bottom of the pan to coat the mixture in the "fond" (the small brown bits that are stuck to the bottom of the skillet, which can deepen the flavor of your stew). Stir in the wine, turn the heat to high, and reduce the mixture until it is basically dry. Add the meat back into the skillet.

Stir in 2 cups of broth and 2 cups of water. Taste the liquid and season with salt and pepper. Next, make the spice satchel by filling a square of cheesecloth with the bay leaf, peppercorns, and sprigs of fresh herbs. Tie with cooking twine, and add the satchel to the stew.

Slow cooking is the key to a tasty stew. Cook at 325°F for 4 hours, stirring occasionally. During the last hour, taste the broth to see if it needs additional seasoning and add salt and pepper accordingly. At this point, add the potatoes, carrots, celery, and corn, then add the peas just before serving. Remove the spice satchel. Ladle up big helpings for you and your guests, and serve with corn bread.

Serves 8

TIP ☞ *Prairie gals threw whatever was available into their stews, so if you have seasonal vegetables lying about, feel free to improvise and throw them into the pot.*

- *Add whole pearl onions instead of chopped onions for a French onion soup effect.*
- *Add dried mushrooms such as porcini or chanterelle (plumped in warm water for 30 minutes) at the same time you add the broth and water for an earthier flavor.*
- *Add a Parmesan cheese rind at the time of the broth and water, and remove before serving.*
- *Add parsnips instead of or in addition to potatoes to give the stew a sweeter, spicier flavor.*
- *Serve the stew up in a bowl topped with sour cream, and serve with corn bread.*

Skillet Corn Bread

WHAT YOU WILL NEED

4 slices bacon, chopped

1 cup yellow cornmeal

2 teaspoons granulated sugar

1 teaspoon salt

1 teaspoon baking powder

¼ teaspoon baking soda

⅓ cup boiling water

¾ cup buttermilk

⅛ to ¼ cup honey, depending on your sweetness preference

1 large egg, lightly beaten

1 jalapeño, finely diced (optional)

Preheat the oven to 450°F. Place the bacon in a 12-inch cast-iron skillet, and render the fat over medium-low heat until the bacon is crisp. Remove the bacon and reserve for another use. Remove all but approximately 2 tablespoons of the fat and reserve for another use.

In a small bowl, combine ⅔ cup of the cornmeal with the sugar, salt, baking powder, and baking soda, and set aside.

TIP *If you don't have a cast-iron skillet, you can use a 9-inch round or square baking pan. Grease lightly with butter or bacon fat, do not preheat the pan, and double the recipe. If you use butter instead of bacon fat, increase the salt to 1½ teaspoons.*

Place the remaining cornmeal in a medium bowl, and pour the boiling water over it. Stir together until you have a stiff mixture (the consistency of grits or polenta), and allow it to cool. Meanwhile, place the hot skillet with the bacon fat into the oven until the fat is crackling hot. Slowly whisk the buttermilk and honey into the cornmeal/water mixture, stirring until the mush is smooth. Whisk an egg into the mush. Fold in the jalapeño.

When the oven is preheated and the skillet is hot, fold the dry ingredients into the wet until the dough is uniformly moistened. Using a sturdy pot holder, carefully remove the skillet from the oven. Tilting the bowl away from yourself, quickly pour the batter into the skillet. Bake about 20 minutes, or until golden brown on the edges and firm to the touch in the center. Remove from the oven and instantly flip the corn bread carefully onto a wire rack. Cool for 5 to 10 minutes and serve.

Makes one 12-inch skillet of corn bread

TIP *Although you can buy preseasoned skillets these days, it is still helpful to know how to season a cast-iron skillet. Wash and thoroughly dry your new skillet. Pour enough oil to liberally cover the surface of your skillet or pan, then place it in the oven at 250°F for several hours. Take it out and wipe out the excess oil. When it is still new, rub it down with oil after each washing. Clean your skillet with hot water and a scrub brush. Do not put it in the dishwasher or use dish soap.*

CURE MEAT

I love cured, salty meats, and I started wondering how on earth to make that particular piece of culinary magic happen in my own home. So I went to a sausage-making and curing class with Chef Gabriel Claycamp, the head chef, instructor, and co-owner of Culinary Communion (www.culinarycommunion.com). I was in hog heaven when I learned, among other things, how to make chorizo and salted air-dried ham (prosciutto).

Dead meat: a corpse.
"Doc Benson came and took care of the dead meat."

TIP *Temperatures warmer than the recommended 50°F to 60°F can cause spoilage during curing. Too low a temperature will interfere with the cure, so add the number of days onto the curing process that your meat fell below the recommended temperature.*

When the curing period is over, brush the meat to remove the excess mixture. Rinse the meat thoroughly (you can soak it in cold water if you like). With some strong cord, hang the meat in a cold place or put it in the refrigerator for at least a week but preferably for three weeks or longer. Enjoy! It'll be worth the wait.

Want to give it a try? Cool temperatures are required when slaughtering, cutting, and curing your meat. Let's assume that you're not butchering your own meat but rather getting a few good cuts from the town's butcher. During and immediately after the curing process (which can take several days or even weeks), place your meats in a cool location (50°F to 60°F is safe).

There are three main ingredients in a short dry cure: salt, which dries out the meat; sugar, which provides flavor and keeps the meat from hardening; and nitrites (also called Tinted Cure Mix [TCM] or Modern Cure), which preserves the color and prevents botulism. There are premixed cures available (online, at a butcher shop, or at a large grocery store) or you can mix your own.

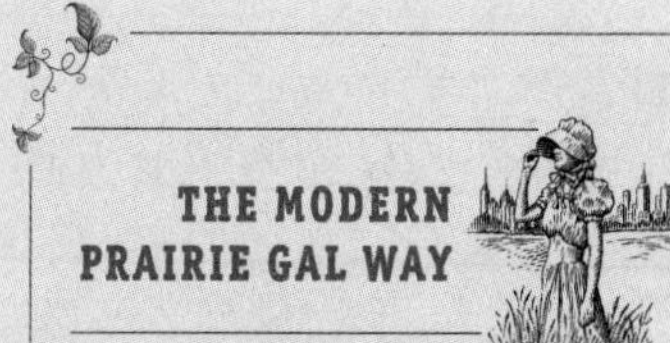

THE MODERN PRAIRIE GAL WAY

Back in the day, whole frontier families got into the spirit and cured a variety of meats in one large batch. But they didn't have fancy contraptions for the process; instead, they used a large hollowed-out log and hung the meat on various hooks in the upright log. They then built and stoked a fire for days, letting the smoke cure and flavor the meat inside the hollow wood (smoke cures are an alternative to sugar cures). This way, they were able to guarantee meat throughout the long winter. Modern prairie gals can smoke meat in electric smokers that can be placed in a garage or on a patio, so there's no need to buy a side of beef to enjoy a little smoked flavor now and again. I'm still suspicious of a smoked Thanksgiving turkey, but I'm told it's delicious.

TIP *Allow enough curing time for the meat to absorb the salt. Keep careful track of the curing time. If you cut it short, the meat may spoil. If you cure too long, the meat loses quality. Keep meat refrigerated or hanging in a cold place (50°F to 60°F) after curing to dry and to give the salt time to spread evenly throughout the meat.*

WHAT YOU WILL NEED

4 pounds kosher salt

1½ pounds white or light brown granulated sugar

1¾ ounces nitrites (TCM or Modern Cure)

25 pounds fresh ham or pork bellies in large hunks or slabs (ask your butcher for large cuts)

Mix the salt, sugar, and nitrites thoroughly in a large bowl. As a general rule, use 1¼ to 1½ ounces of the mixture per pound of ham, and ¾ to 1 ounce of the mixture per pound of bacon. This cure will work for up to 60 pounds of ham or 90 pounds of bacon.

Once the cure is mixed, rub half of the required amount of mixture (based on the meat's size) onto the meat, covering the surface. Put the meat in a pan in the refrigerator or, if the weather is cool enough, in an outside box, barrel, or burlap bag.

Rub the meat with the remaining sugar cure every seven days. Figure on curing the meat for one day for each pound. If you have a 25-pound hunk, cure it for 25 days, rubbing it with the cure on the 7th, 14th, and 21st days. Make sense?

MAKE JUDY'S BREAD-AND-BUTTER PICKLES

When I was just knee-high to a grasshopper, I couldn't stand pickles. I never liked cucumbers, and my mom couldn't fool me. I knew those pickles had once grown plump on the vine as cucumbers. Dill pickles I absolutely refused to touch, and my mom's bread-and-butter pickles just looked mushy and murky in the Ball® jar. But at some point, curiosity got the better of me. Did the pickle taste like bread and/or butter? I lifted out one slice with a fork and nibbled on it. It was unlike anything I'd ever eaten before, and in this case, that was a good thing.

This recipe comes from my mother, a pioneer woman in her own right. This recipe ruined all other pickles for me, and once you sample a jar, you'll see why. (If you want to make more than the yield listed, my mother—with the prudence of a prairie homesteader—suggests reusing the cucumber-onion brine.)

> **Hook, by/on one's own:** on one's own; one's own doing; by one's self.
> *"Since Ma was away visiting kin, Martha put up the preserves on her own hook."*

Place the cucumbers and onions in a large bowl. Sprinkle with the salt and mix. Let stand 3 hours.

Fill a canning kettle (a large pot with a rack inside it) with water and bring to a boil. Turn

WHAT YOU WILL NEED

Canning kettle

4 to 7 canning jars

Large pot

---

1 gallon cucumbers, thinly sliced and unpared

1 quart small onions, thinly sliced

½ cup coarse salt

5 cups vinegar

1 cup water

7 ½ cups sugar

1 teaspoon cinnamon

2 teaspoons celery seed

2 teaspoons mustard seed

2 teaspoons turmeric

the jars upside down, and immerse them on the rack in the kettle.

Pour the vinegar and water into a large pot, and add the sugar, cinnamon, celery seed, mustard seed, and turmeric to create a brine. Bring to a boil. Drain the liquid from the cucumbers and onions, and add them to the brine. Reduce the heat and simmer 3 to 4 minutes.

Pull the jars out of the hot-water bath (use tongs or a dish towel), and fill with pickles immediately (the jars do not have to be completely dry). Ladle or spoon the pickles into the jars, leaving ½ inch of air at the top. Place the canning jar lid over the opening, and screw the ring tightly around the lid. Set the jars on a dry towel away from any drafts (cold air can crack the jars, since they are still very hot). Listen for a pop and look for a depression in the top of the lid while the jars are cooling; this indicates that the jar is safely sealed. Once the jars reach room temperature, store in a cool, dark place for 4 months before opening. Enjoy!

Yields 4 to 7 pints

PREPARE APPLESAUCE

I used to help my mom make applesauce in our 1970s brown-and-orange kitchen, and I remember was how much fun it was to push the mushy fruit through the strainer. It was like magic, but then most things my mother and grandmother cooked up were out of this world.

I got a refresher course from my mom and a few tips from my German sister-in-law Monika. But the real juice came from Dawn Zeligman, an amazing force of nature who does all sorts of prairie-ish activities from her homestead in eastern Michigan.

WHAT YOU WILL NEED

Strainer

Apple peeler, knife, or potato peeler

Potato masher or large spoon

---

4 apples

¼ cup water

2 tablespoons brown sugar

½ teaspoon ground cinnamon

Cardamom, to taste

Gather your apples. Hopefully, you can pick organic apples in an orchard during harvest time. You'll need only a few if you want to make fresh applesauce for dinner or a half-bushel if you are going to be canning your sauce.

Select a mixture of hard and tart apples, such as Granny Smith, Empire, and Gala. Peel and core the apples (old-fashioned crank peelers peel and core at the same time, but you can use a knife or hand-peeler). Dice the apples into chunks (about 1½ inches is good), and put them in a pot with the water. It will seem like there's not enough water but don't worry, there is. Set the temperature to slightly below medium to heat the water.

The apples will start to "weep" (i.e., moisture will start to come out of the fruit). Turn up the heat to medium-high and cover. After 20 minutes, give the apples a stir. Resist the urge to stir them any earlier, as they can burn. The apples should be mushy at this point. Drain and strain them through a strainer, using a potato masher or large spoon to force the fruit through. Only skin should be left in the strainer when done. Add the brown sugar, cinnamon, and cardamom to taste. Let the sauce set for 5 to 10 minutes.

Your applesauce will be light brown. Store-bought applesauce usually contains chemicals to make it a lighter color.

Serves 4

If you want to can your applesauce:

The applesauce is made the same way (although you'll need to increase the ingredients proportionately). Bring a canning kettle filled with water to a boil. Turn the canning jars upside down, and immerse on the rack in the kettle.

Using tongs or a dish towel, pull the jars out of the hot-water bath, and fill them with applesauce immediately, leaving ½ inch of air at the top. Place the canning jar lid over the opening, and screw the ring tightly around the lid. Place the sealed jars on the rack in the boiling water of the kettle so they don't touch the bottom or edges of the kettle. The water should cover the jars by about 1 inch. Leave in the hot-water bath for 15 to 25 minutes, depending on your altitude (the higher, the longer). Remove the jars, setting them on a dry towel away from any drafts (cold air can crack the jars, since they are still very hot). Listen for a pop and look for a depression in the top of the lid while the jars are cooling; this indicates the jar is safely sealed. Once they reach room temperature, store in a cool, dark place.

BAKE A RHUBARB PIE

My grandma had a garden that sat between her farmhouse and our ranch-style home. Cucumbers hid beneath large, leafy umbrellas, berries dotted vines, and carrots announced themselves with lacy stems. Rhubarb wasn't so subtle. It grew up and out, arcing beautifully with its thick, red stalks. I couldn't wait to tuck into a thick slice of a tart rhubarb pie that Grandma would bring over, warm from the oven. I helped her make pies whenever possible. I loved making a mess with the flour and the

Huckleberry above a persimmon: a cut above.
"Sam thought Minnie's pie was a huckleberry above a persimmon, but he couldn't bring himself to tell her so."

dough and then creating order out of the billowy chaos as I rolled out sheets of dough and then turned strips into a basketweave that was as pretty as the pie was delicious.

Several prairie gals (Elise and Dawn, notably) and a resourceful boy named Joel all weighed in with their favorite pie recipes. Here's the result: the perfect rhubarb pie.

The Perfect Lattice-Top Crust

WHAT YOU WILL NEED

In addition to basic mixing bowls, measuring cups and spoons, and various utensils, you'll need:

Food processor, pastry cutter, or large fork

Plastic wrap

Parchment paper

Rolling pin

Pizza wheel or paring knife

Cookie sheet

Pie plate

Pastry brush

2 cups all-purpose unbleached flour (preferably organic)

1 teaspoon salt

2 tablespoons sugar

16 tablespoons (2 sticks) unsalted butter, cut into ½-inch cubes and chilled in the freezer for 30 to 60 minutes

4 tablespoons vegetable shortening, cut into ½-inch cubes and chilled in the freezer for 30 to 60 minutes

8 tablespoons ice water

1 egg yolk

⅛ cup cream or milk

Coarse sugar

The Rhubarb Filling

WHAT YOU WILL NEED

4 cups rhubarb, cut into 1-inch pieces

1¼ cups sugar

⅓ cup flour (unless rhubarb has been harvested early—April, May, June—in which case, cut back by 1 tablespoon flour and substitute 1 tablespoon cornstarch)

Dash of salt (optional)

Cut your rhubarb 4 to 6 hours before making the pie. Refrigerate the fruit for a less "weepy" pie.

Now it's time to make the dough. When measuring the flour, use the "spoon and level" method: Over a paper towel, spoon the flour into a 1-cup measure to overflowing, insert a spoon handle into the cup, and tap the bottom lightly to release any air, then level with a spatula to remove excess.

If you have a food processor, combine the flour, salt, and sugar in the processor bowl fitted with a steel blade. Pulse a few times to evenly distribute the salt and sugar. Sprinkle the butter pieces and vegetable shortening over the flour, then pulse 8 to 10 seconds, or until the mixture has the texture of coarse sand with pea-size bits of butter still visible. Transfer the mixture into a large metal bowl.

If you're working by hand, sift the flour, salt, and sugar together into a large metal bowl to evenly distribute the salt and sugar. Sprinkle the butter pieces and vegetable shortening over the flour, toss with your hands a few times to coat the fat with a bit of flour, then "cut" the fat into the flour by pressing into the bowl with a pastry cutter (preferred) or a large fork (if that's all you've got), until the mixture has the texture of coarse sand with pea-size bits of butter still visible.

Sprinkle 5 tablespoons of the ice water over the mixture, and use a rubber spatula to lift the flour and butter up and over the water. Continue "folding" the mixture in this manner until no more water is visible and it appears to be evenly incorporated into the flour. Add the remaining ice water and repeat "folding" until the mixture just holds together when pressed between your fingers. The dough at this point should feel moist but not sticky.

Turn the dough out onto a clean, dry surface. Gather loose bits and gingerly press so that the mass holds together, then divide into two chunks, one slightly larger than the other. Wrap both tightly in plastic wrap, shape each into a disk, and refrigerate for 1 hour.

Retrieve the dough from the refrigerator. Working with the larger disk first, remove the plastic wrap and place the dough on a large sheet of parchment or plastic wrap, placing another sheet of parchment or plastic wrap on top. Begin rolling, working from the center out and turning the paper ¼ turn every few rolls, eventually achieving a ⅛-inch-thick rectangle, approximately 11 by 15 inches. Place the rolled dough onto a cookie sheet, and remove the top layer of the parchment. Using a pizza wheel or paring knife, trim the edges of the dough to make an even rectangle. Cut the rectangle lengthwise into eight to ten 1- by 15-inch strips, then freeze the strips on the cookie sheet until firm, approximately 30 minutes.

Follow the same rolling method for the smaller piece of dough, forming a round disk instead of a rectangle for the pie's base. Roll the dough to approximately ⅛ inch thick, 12 inches in diameter, and uniformly round. Remove the parchment or plastic wrap, and transfer onto a 9-inch pie plate by rolling the dough loosely around your rolling pin, then unrolling it directly over the pie plate. Gently lift the dough edges with one hand and press into the bottom edge with the other to evenly cover the pie plate surface, then refrigerate.

Now is a good time to preheat your oven to 425°F.

Next, prepare your pie filling. Mix together the rhubarb, sugar, flour, and salt. Pour mixture over the dough in the pie plate, filling to ¼ from the top of the plate. Return the pie plate to the refrigerator.

Remove the other half of dough from the freezer. Beginning on the outer edge of the pie plate, place one strip along the edge with ½-inch overlap. Place another strip at a 90-degree angle. Place a third strip in line with the first, leaving a ¼-inch to ½-inch space between. Then place a fourth strip in line with the second, and continue until you have a complete lattice.

Cut away excess dough around the edges, leaving an overlap of approximately ½ inch all around. With your right hand, spread your index and middle fingers about ¾ inch apart, and press the side of the dough. Using your left index finger, push the dough edge gently between your right fingers. The goal is to use your right hand to push the overlap up onto the rim of the pie plate so that it is not overhanging, but so that it completely covers the surface of the rim. Rotate the pie plate and repeat all the way around.

Whisk the egg yolk in a small bowl with the cream or milk to create an egg wash. Using a pastry brush, brush the tops and edges of the dough with the egg wash, covering the entire crust surfaces (edges and lattice), then sprinkle with coarse sugar.

Place your work of art on a baking sheet and bake until the crust starts to brown, about 25 minutes. Turn the pie half a turn to ensure even cooking, then reduce the oven temperature to 375°F. Continue to bake until the crust reaches a deep golden brown and the filling is bubbling, 25 to 30 minutes more. Remove from the oven and let cool for at least 1 hour before you slice it. Serve with homemade ice cream (see p. 37) for a true rustic indulgence.

TIP☞ *Parchment paper is a way of ensuring even dough that is not overworked. However, if dough stops feeling cold or becomes squishy, put it back in the fridge for 15 minutes until the butter has hardened. If you don't want to use parchment, flour your surface and your rolling pin with just enough flour so the dough doesn't stick; don't overdo it with the flour, or the dough will dry out.*

MAKE ICE CREAM

My favorite ice cream flavor is Blue Moon. I thought everyone knew about the wonder of this creamy flavor that is only surpassed by the remarkable blue color, a color most definitely not found in nature or on the prairie. I was wrong. I was at a chocolate shop in Sarasota, Florida, a few years ago and spotted Blue Moon in the ice cream case. When I ordered it, the salesperson asked me if I was from Michigan. I thought her psychic, but apparently this Florida shop was one of the few places outside the Midwest to carry the ice cream.

WHAT YOU WILL NEED

2 containers, such as 2 different-size coffee cans that have at least a 1-inch gap all around

3 eggs

1 quart half-and-half

3 cups sugar

½ cup flour

½ to 1 teaspoon vanilla extract

1 quart ice (approximately)

1 quart rock salt (approximately)

My dad likes Blue Moon as well, but he has never met an ice cream that he didn't like. It might be that he didn't have a lot of choices growing up. When he was a kid, a local bakery truck made the rounds and sold ice cream to the farming community. Dad would buy a pint of ice cream and gobble it up before it melted. Maybe I inherited my gluttonous ice cream habits from him. Thankfully, now

KEEPING COOL

Ice was a valuable commodity on the prairie—during the summer months, that is. Winters were harsh beyond belief, often reaching temperatures well below zero. It's hard to think that our forefathers cut tunnels through drifts to get from the house, cabin, or shanty to the barn, stable, or lean-to. It's impossible to imagine that kind of cold without Polartec®, let alone electric or gas heat. There were no bubble baths to warm their bones, no electric blanket or heating pad to take the edge off when they climbed into bed.

So pioneers kept warm by doing a lot of physical activity to keep their heart rates up. And if they were near a large frozen lake, the men often trudged out to a particularly choice spot and cut large blocks of ice. They portaged them back to an icehouse and packed the ice tightly together, stuffing sawdust between each layer and between each block. In the summer, no matter the heat, the ice was kept intact in its shelter, until it was time to take out another block, be it for ice cream, ice-cold lemonade, or just to suck on for a reprieve from the heat.

that I have my own ice cream recipe, I don't have to wait for the bakery truck.

With a bit of frontier ingenuity, you can make ice cream in any sort of metal or glass container that will fit inside another can or jar. And once you've mastered this vanilla recipe, feel free to improvise with seasonal fruits, honey, nuts, or other favorite ingredients.

In a mixing bowl, lightly beat the eggs, then stir in the half-and-half, sugar, flour, and vanilla extract. Pour into the smaller container, and securely close the opening (tape down the lid if necessary; you don't want any of the inner goodness to seep out).

Place the smaller container inside the larger one. Alternating several layers of ice and rock salt, pack the space around the small container. Close the opening of the larger container securely.

Now the fun really begins. Vigorously roll, kick, or shake your container. After 20 minutes, carefully remove both lids and check the consistency of your ice cream. If it's not yet frozen, close the inner lid, drain off the liquid in the outer container, and add more ice and rock salt. After 10 more minutes, check your ice cream. When it reaches a consistency you fancy, scoop it out, sprinkle some fresh berries on top, and enjoy the fruit of your labors.

Yields 2 quarts

SWEET TREAT CHERRIES

Growing up on a farm, I never had far to look when I wanted something sweet. I only had to go downstairs and pull a jar of canned fruit. And I love all things cherry, especially cherry pie. Use these cherries in pie or on vanilla ice cream (pit them first), or just pop them as a treat when you are craving something sweet.

Corned: drunk.

"Ella was tempted to try some brandied cherries but she was afraid of getting corned."

WHAT YOU WILL NEED

Canning kettle

6 canning jars

---

6 to 8 pounds dark sweet cherries, cleaned and destemmed

2 cups sugar

4 cups water

Place the sugar and water in a saucepan and bring to a boil until the sugar is dissolved. Let cool.

Bring a canning kettle filled with water to a boil. Turn the jars upside down, and immerse on the rack in the kettle.

Pull the jars out of the hot-water bath (use tongs or a dish towel). Pack them with cherries (pit if you plan to use cherries for pie) to the rim of each jar, leaving a bit of airspace. Pour the syrup into the jar, also to the rim, leaving some space at the top. Place the canning jar lid over the opening, and screw the ring tightly around the lid.

Place the sealed jars on the rack in the boiling water of the kettle so they don't touch the bottom or edges of the kettle. The water should cover the jars by about 1 inch. Leave in the hot-water bath for 25 to 45 minutes, depending on your altitude (the higher, the longer). Remove the jars, setting them on a dry towel away from any drafts (cold air can crack the jars, since they are still very hot). Listen for a pop and look for a depression in the top of the lid while the jars are cooling; this indicates the jar is safely sealed. Once they reach room temperature, store in a dark, cool place, and let them set for 6 months or longer.

Yields 6 pints

MAKE DANDELION GREENS

My grandma, a thrifty farmwife, had reputedly made more than one dinner dish using the flora and fauna available around the farm. That meant everything was fair game. I was happy to sample the jam made from the raspberry bushes that grew next to the shed. I helped her pick wild asparagus that poked out from under the apple trees across the street. And then there were dandelions. Dandelions! They were weeds we constantly battled on the front lawn and in the large field next to our house. I mowed down scores of the cheery yellow weed; I couldn't believe they could be used to make soup, greens, and even wine. My grandma's forays into dandelion delicacies were nothing compared with her friends. Down the road, Harry Beckadam made elderberry wine. Marvel Gordon was known to throw roadkill in a pot for dinner. When I heard about these delicacies, Grandma's experiments didn't sound so bad.

> **Trace:** a trail or path.
> *"Catherine liked to follow the trace to her favorite meadow, which was dotted by wildflowers all summer long."*

And heck, Grandma made stuff with weeds, and as a self-respecting curious kid, I wasn't about to turn away a plate of down-home cooking. As an adventurous adult, not much has changed, except that I can now make my own version at home. It's surprisingly easy. My

WHAT YOU WILL NEED

Saucepan

1 pound dandelion greens
1 teaspoon salt
1 clove garlic, minced
½ cup onion, chopped
¼ cup olive oil
salt and pepper, to taste
½ cup romano cheese, grated

grandpa fancied dandelion greens; here's a variation on his salted and boiled recipe.

Discard dandelion stems and buds, keeping only the leaves. Wash greens thoroughly and soak with salt in water. Cut the leaves into 2-inch pieces and add to a saucepan with ½ cup salted water. Cook them uncovered, over medium heat, about 10 minutes, or until tender.

Sauté garlic and onion in a skillet with olive oil. Drain greens and add to skillet. Salt and pepper to taste. Sprinkle grated romano cheese over each serving.

Serves 4

Horn: a glass of liquor or ale. *"Harry didn't think that a horn now and again would do any harm."*

TIP *Serve with a rustic meat or poultry dish, such as roast chicken.*

STEEP THE PERFECT POT OF TEA

For 30-some years, I declined to drink coffee. I think my aversion came from sampling my dad's or grandmother's cup of black coffee, which I still can't stomach. However, I needed a warm drink during cold Michigan winters, so I turned to tea. My early tea experiences included a Lipton® teabag and a liberal spoonful of sugar. No milk, no fancy-pants herbal tea for me. A strong, sweetened black tea did wonders for my spirit.

Today, I enjoy a variety of those fancy-pants herbal and green teas. I've sampled various teas, from Darjeeling to oolong to jasmine to lavender-chamomile to the more exotic blends from far-flung locales. But it's always nice to come back to a properly made pot of black tea.

PERCOLATING ON THE PRAIRIE

Prairie gals didn't have the benefit of over-the-counter stimulants. And even if a shopkeeper recommended something to perk them up, they wouldn't think of spending a hard-won penny on such an extravagance.

Sunshine, strong tea (some using prairie grass), and various coffee concoctions (some using chicory) were all natural stimulants to keep energy up during long days of chores. Even though the coffee percolator was patented in 1865, most settlers didn't have fancy coffeemakers in their claim shanties. Rather, they put coffee grounds and water into an enamel kettle and boiled it. The grounds would somewhat settle as a prairie woman poured herself a steaming cup of rustic coffee.

WHAT YOU WILL NEED

Ceramic or china teapot

Teakettle or saucepan

Tea cozy

Tea strainer

Cup and saucer, for each person

Water

Loose black tea

Sugar

Milk, to taste

Pour hot water into a ceramic or china teapot and put the lid back on. This heats the teapot and prepares it for your tea. In a teakettle or pan, bring cold water to a boil.

Discard the water in the now-heated teapot and add your tea to the empty pot. Use 3 teaspoons of tea per person and 1 extra teaspoon for the pot. So for two people, scoop in 7 teaspoons. Now, pour the boiling water into the teapot and over the tea leaves. Put the lid back on, and cover the pot with a tea cozy. Steep (that is, let it sit) for 5 minutes.

At this point, pour the tea through a tea strainer into a cup (with a saucer). If you want to read tea leaves, do not strain the tea. If you are using a strong black tea, add 3½ teaspoons of sugar and a dollop of milk. Stir and drink. You can also add sugar and milk to taste. For your second cup, you might need to add more sugar and milk, as the tea will have continued to "stew" under the cozy.

TIP☞ *Do not drink tea after 5 p.m. Strong tea is high in caffeine and can disrupt your sleep.*

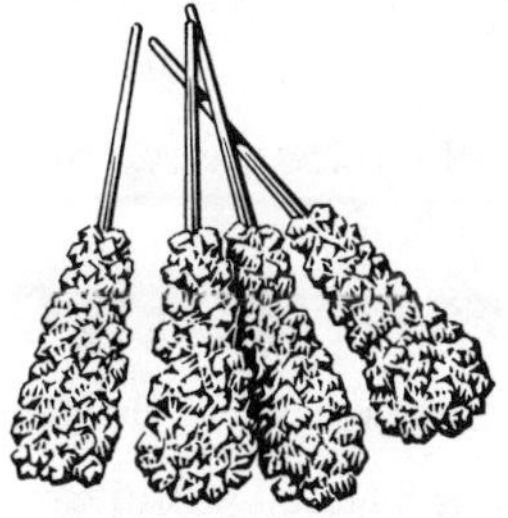

MAKE ROCK CANDY

My family vacations often consisted of five people and as many suitcases crammed into a station wagon driving down old highways next to train tracks. My dad is a hard-core train enthusiast. I was not so enthused. But my dad managed to pique my interest by making a game out of train spotting. He told my brothers and me that whoever spotted the train first would get money. How much money was determined by how rare the engine was. Sometimes I'd score a dime, other times a silver dollar.

> **Big bugs:**
> bigwigs; important people.
> *"When big bugs passed through town, all the townsfolk put on their Sunday best and sent out invitations for tea."*

At tourist attractions and along the highway, we'd stop at gift shops. Many of them had a general store or trading post theme, and there was always something for which I wanted to trade my newly earned silver dollar: a black-and-white cuff at the Continental Divide, a blue coral necklace in New Mexico, silver charms for my charm bracelet pretty much everywhere, a T-shirt in Iowa.

Some things didn't last nearly as long as my jewelry and T-shirt purchases. Candy, for instance. I was charmed by the novelty of rock candy. Like the different flavored jars of candy canes I'd see near the counter, rock candy was a throwback to simpler times. And what kid doesn't like food on a stick? When I learned how to make rock candy, I realized why it was so popular long ago. It's super easy and doesn't require a lot of special tools. And it's just plumb fascinating.

WHAT YOU WILL NEED

Clean glass jar

6-inch ice cream sticks

Pencil

Tape

4 cups sugar

1 cup water

Food coloring

In a saucepan, heat (but do not boil) 2 cups of the sugar and the water. Stir slowly until the sugar is completely dissolved. Gradually add a few drops of food coloring—your choice—and the remaining sugar, stirring continuously until all the sugar is dissolved.

Pour your colorful sugar water into a clean glass jar. Tape the sticks to a pencil and suspend them across the mouth of the jar so that the ends hang into the liquid.

All on one stick:
a conglomeration or combination.
"She opened a candy shop and tea house, all on one stick."

Crystals suitable to eat will form in an hour and continue to grow for several days to a week. Pieces can be broken off and eaten after the first hour, but try to resist the urge to suck on them. Although you may see modest results quickly, larger rock-candy crystals will take time to form. Good things come to those who wait, and pretty sticks of candy are yours to be had if you show a bit of patience.

Yields 12 ounces

MAKE POPCORN BALLS

Popcorn was a special treat on the prairie, and that sense of occasion was still present by the time my family was plugging in aerodynamic air poppers. We also had a popcorn machine that looked like a wok with a tightly fitting yellow plastic dome over it. Add a little oil, let the corn do its thing, and then flip both pieces over so the dome becomes the bowl. It was genius. But around the time aerobics and Richard Simmons were sweeping the nation, we put that pop-

per in the back of a cupboard and plugged in the air popper. I like my popcorn covered in delicious goo, so I put butter in the warming tray on top. It had little holes in it that would drip onto the corn as it came through the chute.

But the classic way to make popcorn is just with a standard iron skillet, and my dad loved to do it up old school every now and then. Aside from a few burnt kernels, the skillet popcorn was both rustic and decadent. However you choose to pop the corn, popcorn balls make a festive treat at the holidays or anytime else during the year.

WHAT YOU WILL NEED

Candy thermometer

¼ cup unpopped popcorn
2 tablespoons vegetable oil
¼ cup butter
½ teaspoon salt
1 cup granulated sugar
⅓ cup light corn syrup
⅓ cup water

Set your oven to 200°F.

Pop the popcorn however you choose. To do it on the stove, add the vegetable oil to a sturdy pan, pot, or skillet, and heat to medium-high. Spread the popcorn evenly over the bottom of the pan and cover with a lid. When it starts to pop, turn the heat to high. The corn will really start popping. Give the pan a gentle shake while the popcorn is going crazy to redistribute the unpopped kernels. When you only hear one pop at a time, quickly remove the pan and lid, and pour the popcorn into a large pan. Place your pan into the oven.

Now, let's make syrup. Put the butter, salt, sugar, corn syrup, and water in a medium saucepan over medium heat and stir. When the mixture starts to boil, stop stirring and let the syrup cook. When the temperature reaches 270°F, it's time to have a ball. (If you don't have a candy thermometer handy, drop a spoonful of syrup into a cup of cold water. If it turns into hard, stringy-looking pieces, it's ready to go.)

Remove the pan from heat and remove your popcorn from the oven. Slowly pour the syrup over the popcorn, stirring until all the kernels are coated. Test the popcorn's temperature by picking up a few pieces. When the popcorn is cool enough to handle, coat your hands with a bit of butter and then form the popcorn into large balls. Set on wax paper or in a clean pan to cool. Eat up.

Yields 10 large popcorn balls

THE MODERN PRAIRIE GAL WAY

During cozy nights in the homestead, it wasn't unheard of to find prairie gals pouring hot molasses over popcorn and quickly shaping the sticky corn into balls. While popcorn seems like a modern miracle, popcorn and popcorn balls were popular treats on the prairie, but settlers didn't always stick to molasses when coating their popcorn. They flavored their treats with rose, peppermint, honey, and vanilla. If you're feeling like a bit of a popcorn pioneer, pick one of your favorite flavors (or even your favorite food coloring) and work it into the mixture. For a homespun gift, create an assortment of flavored popcorn balls and wrap them in cellophane. Rustic, perhaps. Tasty, definitely.

GATHERINGS

TEA PARTY

Little girls aren't the only ones who should have tea parties. Consider gathering a group of your most genteel chums over for a proper tea. But rather than a stuffy English high tea experience, make your party decidedly less refined (and therefore more fun).

Cover your table with a gingham tablecloth, set out cups and saucers, and create a welcoming spread of snacks, both sweet and savory.

Make your food in advance so you'll be able to enjoy your guests. Make egg salad, cucumber, and watercress sandwiches (with crusts cut off, of course), like a proper young lady. Whip up a pie (may I suggest rhubarb, as on p. 31) or a comforting cobbler. Serve seasonal fruit, and adorn your table with unused canning jars filled with seasonal herbs or wildflowers.

Consider conducting a "tea tasting" so your friends can sample some blends other than the usual box of Earl Grey they pick up at the local grocery. Seek out a shop that specializes in tea for a few unusual blends, or visit a health-food store for additional choices.

Brew and steep several pots of tea (see p. 43 for steeping the perfect pot of tea) right before your guests are ready to sit down. Pour rounds of different teas (such as black teas like Darjeeling, Earl Grey, Assam, and Ceylon) so guests can try one blend at a time. Serve with sugar, milk, lemon wedges, and honey.

For a fun activity, try reading each other's tea leaves. Do not strain the tea as you pour it into a cup. When your guest has only a small amount of liquid left in her cup, ask her to hold it in her left hand and swirl three times clockwise. She should then place the cup upside down on her saucer. After several seconds, she should turn the cup right side up and set it on the saucer with the handle facing the tea-leaf reader.

Chances are, you probably don't have actual training in tasseography (tea-leaf reading), so you can just look for images (much like cloud formations) and interpret them how you see fit for maximum fun. For instance, an airplane could suggest a trip or being up in the air. An owl could indicate wisdom or gossip.

Send guests home with a bag of tea, a strainer, or a tea ball as a party favor.

Necessary: euphemism for the outhouse or water closet; the bathroom.

"Betty had to excuse herself to go to the necessary."

THE BATHROOM

Most prairie dwellings had only an outhouse out back, but pioneers found lots of ways to spruce and freshen up. Luckily, by the time I rolled around, my family's "homestead" had indoor plumbing and a hot-water heater.

Prairie gals knew the value of a good hot bath heated with a steaming kettle of water, particularly after a long day venturing in the wild, even if they couldn't enjoy leisurely soaks. What I learned from those prairie gals who came before was to value my precious, sometimes limited time in the bathroom.

When I was able to loiter in the bathtub, I did it up right. I poured in bubble bath, bath salts, and bath oils (usually not at the same time). I experimented with egg-white facials and mayonnaise hair treatments. And I read in the bath, books about little houses and big woods.

I've found comfort in those welcoming waters for many years. Whenever I'm stressed, I enter the bathroom and close the door on the world. While I'm a prairie girl at the core, I enjoy the modern luxury of letting the water run until it warms me again.

EMBROIDER TOWELS

There were two kinds of towels in my house: the towels we used and the towels we hung on the rack when guests came, and never the two would meet. The towels we used were usually threadbare and faded from repeated washings. But the guest towels! They were stitched with flowers, mushrooms, or holiday wreaths, all worked in metallic thread. They had fringe that looked neat and uniform, not mangy and gap-toothed. Mom sometimes got creative and folded a guest hand towel on the basin next to the dish of tiny guest soaps.

I decided to make my own adorable embroidered towels for my very own use, choosing a design that was appealing to me. You, too, can embellish your own towels, or use the delightful haystack design to spruce up curtains, handkerchiefs, clothing, or place mats.

I offer some basic instructions for embroidery in the Bedroom chapter (see pp. 102–107), so I thought I'd provide a different stitch option here to create a charming hand towel to put out for guests or just anytime you're feeling the need to spruce up your claim shanty.

WHAT YOU WILL NEED

Size 18 to 22 embroidery needle (any size sharp needle will do, as long as you can thread embroidery floss through it and pass it through your towel)

Cotton embroidery floss

4- to 7-inch embroidery hoop

Small pair of sharp scissors

Hand towel with a smooth band (pass your needle through the fabric before beginning to make sure that the weave is not too tight)

Dressmaker's carbon paper with pencil, or transfer pencil

Prewash your towel. Make sure you purchase one that has a smooth band suitable for embroidery. It's trickier to stitch evenly when the towel is plush.

Follow the directions on p. 103 to transfer the pattern onto your towel. Once you've got your design in place, make the towel taut by first separating the two embroidery hoops. Lay the towel so the design is within the inner, nonadjustable hoop. Place the adjustable hoop over and around these, and press down. Pull your fabric taut like a drum, and tighten the hoop's screw. Retighten and readjust the fabric and hoop as you embroider as needed. Whenever you put down your work for any long periods of time, loosen the screws and let your embroidery breathe.

Cut a piece of floss about 12 inches long (one long strand can become tangled or unwieldy), and thread it through your needle. Pull a few inches through (enough so that your floss won't come off the needle), and make a knot an inch or two from the longer end.

Starting from the back of your fabric (which should feature your design tracing), bring your needle through the fabric from back to front

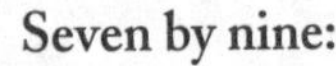

Seven by nine: something or someone of inferior or common quality, originating from common windowpanes of that size. *"The handwork on Lily's towel was very seven by nine, and her mother suggested she have it remade."*

and pull the floss through until the knot touches the fabric. Staying on the tracing, pass the needle back through the fabric ¼ to ⅛ of an inch away from your knot. Hurray! You've just embroidered your first stitch.

For this project, you will use a **chain stitch**. Bring the floss to the right side (the side that you want to show) of the towel. Assuming you are holding the needle in your right hand, hold the floss down with your left thumb as you stitch into the same hole you just came out of. Do not pull tightly. Instead, leave a small loop of floss on the right side of the towel. Bring the needle up through the fabric about ⅛ inch forward on your tracing, coming up through the loop. Bring the floss over the loop, and create another loop that overlaps the previous one (see the illustration at left). Continue in this manner until you finish your design. If you run out of floss, leave a tail long enough to weave through the back of your stitches when done. Change floss colors as necessary, threading the needle and knotting the floss just as you did initially.

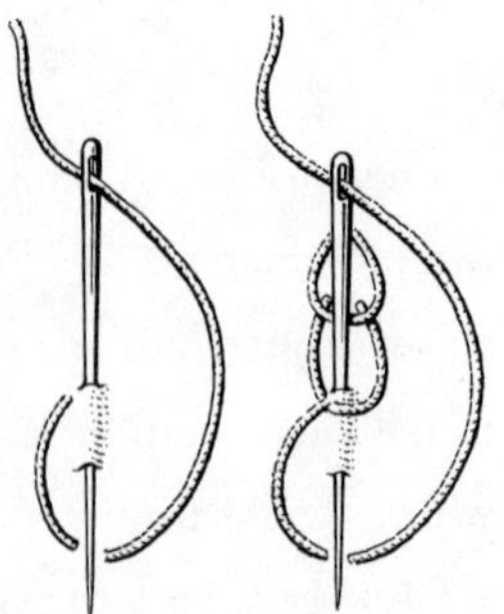

MIX A ROSEWATER SPRITZER

As much as I hanker for days of yore, the issue of hygiene stops me in my tracks. I like my face and body products, not to mention cosmetics. Back in the day, I would have been branded a harlot. In theory, I like the idea of the natural, no-makeup gal, but it's just not me.

Throughout my adolescence and college, I experimented with different types of makeup and facial products, from that robin's egg blue eyeliner I purchased at Woolworth's to tubs of Noxzema® and later to Clinique®'s three-step skin-care program.

But these days, I'm downsizing in all areas of my life, including my toilette. I've started whipping up my own products, which not only saves my pennies for a rainy day but also satisfies my pioneer spirit. This rosewater spritzer is both refreshing and genteel. I find it ladylike, dear, and reminiscent of the women who came before me. And if that's not enough incentive to whip this up, how about this: It's easy as pie.

WHAT YOU WILL NEED

Glass mason jar

Glass or plastic spray bottle

⅔ cup rosewater (you'll need a handful of dried rose petals for this)

⅓ cup witch hazel

6 drops rose essential oil

First, you need to make rosewater, which sounds way more complicated than it actually is. Sterilize a glass mason jar in boiling water and allow it to dry. Place a handful of dried rose petals in the jar, cover with boiling water, seal, and leave for 24 hours. Strain the liquid, discard the petals, and—*voilà*—you have rosewater. You could put this in a pretty glass bottle and use it by itself as a refreshing toner. Give a bottle as a gift and your friend will be dazzled.

Continuing on to make the spritzer, sterilize a glass or plastic spray bottle. When dry, pour in the witch hazel and rosewater, and shake to blend. Add the rose oil. Shake well, hold the bottle about 6 inches from your face, and spray lightly. That's it! Refrigerate the bottle between uses. It will keep the mixture fresh and provide an even more invigorating experience when you spritz it on your face.

Yields 1 cup

BRAID HAIR AND MAKE A BUN FIT FOR ANY BONNET

I haven't had long hair since my mom bent me over the sink and washed my hair with Johnson's® Baby Shampoo. I had thick, golden locks that she used to brush into adorable ponytails on either side of my head. I looked a bit like Cindy Brady, and I mean that in a good way.

> Wrathy: angry.
> *"It made Nina quite wrathy when Jesse pulled her plaits during school."*

Then I traded in classic long hair for trendy hairdos. Since it was the '80s and I was in my teens, you can only imagine the permed, red Bozo hair I was sporting. It was as far from the prairie as you can possibly get. Then I refined my look and adopted a sleek, flat-ironed career style. But recently, I've let my hair grow. It's long and lustrous, but it gets in the way, so I need to pin it back and put it up. Why not in a useful and utilitarian braid?

THE MODERN PRAIRIE GAL WAY

Tomboys on the prairie found braids very useful. Pigtails kept long hair out of the way, when girls were kicking a ball around the schoolyard, chasing after their ponies, or simply trudging through chores. But when they finally noticed that boys weren't so bad after all, the tomboy was eager to transform into a young lady. This meant pinning her plaits up into a ladylike bun. Even today, a bun looks sophisticated and is likely to attract the attention of eligible young men. For a modern twist, add some ribbon or fun hair clips.

Updos and plaited hair may seem too much of a bother to a modern gal, but they were a part of a frontier gal's daily life. Tight braids were practical: They kept a girl's crowning glory out of the way during chores, field work, and homework.

Today, pigtails are a playful option, and buns still look womanly and elegant. While bonnets may not exactly be in fashion, braids still look great with bucket hats and newsboy caps. Which just goes to show that those pioneers were way ahead of their time.

WHAT YOU WILL NEED

BRAIDS:
Hair
(should be at
least shoulder length)

Hair elastics
(two for pigtails,
one for a single plait)

Ribbon (optional)

BUN:
Hair
(should be at
least shoulder length)

Bobby pins

To make pigtails, part your hair from your forehead to the nape of your neck, and make two loose, low ponytails behind your ears. Taking one ponytail at a time, divide the hair into three equal sections. Grasp the three pieces close to the head. Two pieces should be in your left hand and divided by your index finger, and the third piece should be in your right hand. Lay the right section over the center section (it now becomes the center piece) and then the leftmost section over the center section (it now becomes the center piece). Continue alternating the right and left sections over the center section until you come to the ends of your hair. Secure with an elastic band and repeat the process on the other side.

To make one braid down your back, pull your hair into a low ponytail at the nape of your neck. But do not secure with an elastic band; just hold it in your hand. Divide the ponytail into three sections, and braid the hair in a similar fashion as for the pigtails above.

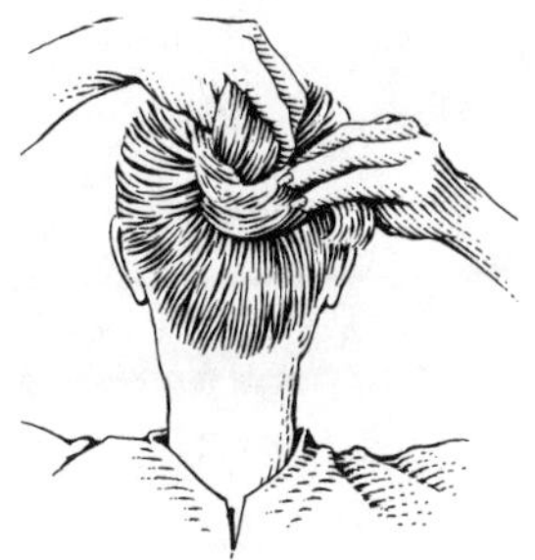

If you want to graduate to a bun, here's how to do it with minimum fuss. Pull your hair into a low ponytail at the nape of the neck. Secure with an elastic band. Now twist your hair clockwise around the ponytail elastic, securing it with bobby pins every ½ inch or so. You can try tucking the ends under the elastic or secure with bobby pins. Finish with hairspray to set the look.

MAKE A POULTICE

Prairie gals had to ward off sickness, cuts, and diseases during their vigorous and sometimes uncertain life in the wild. They didn't always have medical help or medication, so they had to make do. Often ingenious and always crafty, those pioneers had a plethora of natural concoctions for whatever ailed them. They mixed up pastes and teas made from things foraged from the wilderness. Today, that wilderness might just be the aisles of a health-food store, but you can still heal yourself with a bit of moxie and a handful of herbs.

If you're unfamiliar with them, poultices are pastes made from crushed herbs that are used to treat various conditions.

WHAT YOU WILL NEED

Clean cloth
(gauze, linen, muslin)

Herbs or produce as specified
(see below for specifics)

Rolling pin

Wool cloth

Clip, safety pin, or bandage

Start by assessing your physical ailment. For our purposes, let's cover congestion, skin irritation, and bruising.

A basic poultice technique: Wrap your herbs in a clean cloth, folding it so the herbs are secured in a pocket of sorts. Next, crush the herbs by rolling your pin over the cloth. Unfold and apply the pulp directly to the affected area. Place the cloth over the herbs, and wrap it onto the skin with a hot, moist wool cloth. Secure with a clip or bandage. Leave in place 20 minutes to overnight, as long as it feels soothing.

Potato Poultice

WHAT YOU WILL NEED
(IN ADDITION TO THE ABOVE)

Pot

2 unpeeled potatoes, diced in
1-inch cubes

For congestion, arthritis, and eczema, you can make this poultice in a jiffy. Put the potatoes in a pot, cover with water, bring to a boil, and let boil until they're tender (they should break apart when you stick a fork in them). Drain and mash the potatoes. Spread the spuds onto the center of a clean cloth, and fold it up. Let the potatoes cool slightly, then apply the poultice to the affected skin. Cover the poultice with a hot, moist wool cloth or towel, and secure in place with a safety pin or clip. Remove the concoction when it's cold or becomes uncomfortable.

Garlic-Mustard Poultice

WHAT YOU WILL NEED (IN ADDITION TO THE THINGS AT LEFT)

4 cloves garlic

¼ cup crushed mustard seeds

Garlic and mustard not only zest up your dinner but also can clear out your lungs. Peel, then crush or press the garlic and mix it with the mustard seed. Place it in a clean cloth, fold up the cloth, and apply to the chest or back. Wring out a steaming-hot towel, and wrap it around the mixture and cloth to secure in place. Breathe deeply. Remove when the poultice becomes cold or uncomfortable.

Comfrey Poultice

WHAT YOU WILL NEED (IN ADDITION TO THE THINGS AT LEFT)

Pestle & saucepan

3 tablespoons fresh comfrey

¼ cup water

For cuts, bruises, sprains, and even broken bones, consider a comforting comfrey poultice. Using a pestle, grind the comfrey into a paste in mortar. Put it in a small saucepan with the water and bring to a slow, roiling boil. Let the mixture simmer until it becomes a sticky paste. Allow it cool slightly, then spread the paste onto the center of a clean cloth. Place the mixture and cloth onto the injured area and wrap a moist, hot towel around them, securing it in place with a clip or safety pin. Leave on overnight. Repeat as needed for relief.

BATHE YOUR PET, WHATEVER IT MAY BE

Prairie lasses frequently had to bathe not only themselves but also numerous farm animals and pets. Trying to wrangle our dog, Tippy, into the bathtub was always a chore; Tippy was an indoor/outdoor mutt, which meant that she often tracked in assorted organic material. We had better luck hosing her down outside, but that typically resulted in her rolling around in the nearest puddle or pile of dirt. If we managed to actually give her a proper bath, she usually shook and sprayed everyone in a 10-foot radius.

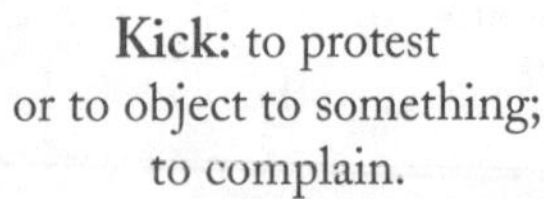

Kick: to protest or to object to something; to complain.
"Prince did his best not to kick when Clarissa soaped the horse up."

The same levels of patience and control apply when washing a larger animal. Some things never change: On the prairie, a firm and loving hand also went a long way to keeping a pet or livestock clean and happy...and keeping your distance from a wet pet kept you dry.

Smallish Pets

WHAT YOU WILL NEED

- Pet brush
- Tub or large basin
- Rubber mat
- Lukewarm water
- Animal-approved shampoo
- Bowl or measuring cup
- Pet conditioner (optional)
- Several large, dry towels

Brush your pet's coat thoroughly before you attempt to give it a bath. Place a rubber mat in a tub or large basin to prevent slipping. If you are using a tub or shower stall, put a screen over the drain to catch fur. Wear old clothes, as your pet isn't the only one likely to get wet during the experience.

Fill the tub with warm water; the temperature should be warm—not hot—when you test it with your elbow. Carefully place your pet in the tub, and let it get acclimated to the temperature and sensation.

Shampoo your pet's head, taking care to avoid ears, eyes, and mouth. Work your way down to the paws and tail. Rinse thoroughly by pouring fresh warm water over your pet's coat with a measuring cup or bowl; if using a spray nozzle, rinse your animal, avoiding the head and genitals. If you like, apply a pet conditioner at this time, again starting with the head and working your way to the tail. Rinse thoroughly.

Place a large towel on the floor. With both hands, open another towel, wrap your pet in it, and pull your wet one out of the bath and onto the towel on the floor. Vigorously rub your pet, taking care with the head and genital area. Get as much water out of your pet's coat, so when it shakes, you won't be sprayed.

If your pet is short-haired, brush the fur out with a pet comb or brush. If the fur is longer, let the fur dry before attempting to brush it out. Turn up the heat or place your pet near a heat source (like a cozy fireplace), and create a bed for it with a warm blanket. If your pet goes outdoors to do its business, keep it on a leash until it's fully dry.

TIP ☞ *Washing your pet too often can result in a dry, itchy coat and skin.*

Livestock and Large Pets

WHAT YOU WILL NEED

Hose
Restraint
Sponge
Animal-friendly shampoo
Water
Brush
Comb

First, put your animal in a halter, yoke, or other suitable restraint and secure it outside near a water hose. Turn on the hose and adjust so it is gentle and the temperature is warm. Rinse your animal.

Starting from the ground up, use a soft sponge to soap up its feet/hooves and legs. Work from the belly to the back and from the head to the tail.

TIP *Do not wash your animal if the temperature dips below 65°F.*

Take care not to soap the face. Holding or stroking its head with one hand, a soft rinse with clean water should do the trick with their head. Avoid the eyes, ears, and mouth as best you can. If the animal gets uppity, hold its restraint and quickly finish with that area. When you reach the tail, gently pull it up and wash the genital area.

Rinse the animal well with a gentle, warm spray. Brush and comb the animal downward and then forward, working your way from head to tail. If it's warm and sunny, let the animal dry thoroughly in the sun before putting it back in its stall. Keep it away from mud!

MAKE SOAP

A strapping young man once told me how to create soap by making lye from ashes and rendering fat from butchered animals. I thought him rather, well, nutty. Can you imagine my surprise and delight to discover that the same technique was used by prairie folk? I confess that I swooned. I've never tried this soapmaking method, but it's nice to know that in a pinch, you can make lemonade out of lemons, or in this case, cleanliness out of filth.

While there are many ways to make soap, I'm going to show you a cold-process method, which is what it says: a way of making soap without an external heat source (although you have to heat up the oils). Many ingredients are used in soaps, but I tried to keep the materials simple, using items you can find locally in health-food stores, grocery and craft stores, and perhaps even hardware stores (for lye).

TIP *When working with lye, wear goggles, rubber gloves, and clothing that will cover your skin (even when cleaning your supplies). Keep lye away from your skin, as well as from kids and pets. If you do come into contact with lye, rinse the area with vinegar and wash your skin well with soap and water. Other tips for working with lye:*

- *Do not use lye containers and utensils for anything other than lye.*
- *Always add lye to water, not the other way around.*
- *Work in a ventilated area and take care not to inhale lye powder when pouring.*
- *Measure your lye very carefully, as just one ounce will throw off the recipe, and not in a good way.*

It may look like a long list of supplies but most of the items are not expensive, and once you've put together your soap "pantry," you'll be set up to host a soapmaking party (see p. 80) or simply whip up soap on a whim.

WHAT YOU WILL NEED

Equipment (earmark these items for soapmaking only):

Soap mold (you can make a mold from all sorts of containers, such as a rubber container, thick cardboard box, even an ice cube tray; look for things that are flexible that you can gently twist to remove the soap)

Waxed paper for lining the mold

Scale (with ounces and grams, if possible—most soapmaking recipes measure out ingredients in ounces)

Saucepan for heating the oils

Two candy thermometers (one for your oil mixture and one for your lye solution)

Goggles and rubber gloves

4- to 6-cup stainless-steel or glass container for mixing lye and water (do not use aluminum, tin, or thin plastic)

Sturdy rubber spatula or wooden spoons

Large stainless-steel, enamel, or plastic heat-resistant pot for mixing the soap

Old towel or blanket

Ingredients:

2.4 ounces sweet almond oil

4.0 ounces coconut oil

5.8 ounces grapeseed oil

2.4 ounces olive oil

2.4 ounces palm oil

2.4 ounces lye (i.e., sodium hydroxide)

5.7 ounces water

2 teaspoons essential oil

THE MODERN PRAIRIE GAL WAY

When I think about how adventurous prairie gals were when roaming the woods or the prairie, I can only imagine how difficult it was to keep dresses and petticoats clean of mud and grass stains. More than once, I suspect a gal tried to hide her disarray behind an apron or coat, perhaps even with a well-placed patch or trim. Today, when I inadvertently spill or stain my clothes, I artfully reposition a broach, turn back a cuff, or otherwise mask the mark until I can go at it in the laundry room.

First, clean and line your mold with waxed paper.

Weigh your oils, then combine them (except the essential oil) in a saucepan and melt over low heat. When the temperature reaches 100°F to 125°F—check by dipping a candy thermometer into the pan—the oils are ready. Set aside.

Put on your goggles and gloves and keep them on throughout the process. Now, weigh your lye and water, taking care to be precise. Add the lye into the water slowly, stirring constantly. Do not lean over the lye solution and do not let lye granules cake on or stick to the bottom of the bowl. When the temperature cools to 100°F to 125°F, the solution is ready.

TIP *Wrapping a bar in waxed paper and tying it with a dainty ribbon makes for a charming gift.*

Mix the melted oils and lye solution together in a new container. Stir with a rubber spatula or wooden spoon until "tracing" occurs. Tracing is the point when the soap from the spatula leaves a trail when drizzled over the mixture.

Add the essential oil and stir. Promptly pour the mixture into your mold. Wrap an old towel or blanket around the mold. Allow 48 hours for the mold to set, then remove your soap from the mold and slice into bars (1 inch thick is good). At this point, the bars need to cure (like smoked meat). This takes around two weeks (the longer you let the soap cure, the harder it will become). When the soap seems relatively firm, test a bar by washing your hands. If it doesn't seem drying or irritating, feel free to lather up everywhere else.

MIX A LEMON VERBENA COLOGNE

I took a shine to Jean Naté® when I was a young miss. It was an "after-bath splash" and I doused myself in it. It felt fresh, tart, and cool. While I have dabbled with other scents and potions, I always come back to citrus scents. They perk me up, no matter my mood or energy level.

WHAT YOU WILL NEED

2 glass bottles with lids or stoppers

1 tablespoon lemon peel, finely chopped

1 tablespoon orange peel, finely chopped

3 tablespoons vodka, 100 proof

Sieve or cheesecloth

5 drops orange essential oil

5 drops lemon essential oil

5 drops grapefruit essential oil

1 cup distilled water

Sterilize a glass bottle and lid or stopper in a boiling hot-water bath and let dry. Place the peels and vodka in the bottle. Seal tightly and set it in a cool, dark place for one week.

At the end of the week, pour the liquid through a fine sieve or cheesecloth into another clean jar or glass. Resterilize your original bottle and lid. Now pour your juiced-up vodka (do not drink it!) back into the bottle and add your essential oils and distilled water. Let it sit in a cool, dark place such as a closet or even the refrigerator for two weeks (check on it every so often and give it a good shake). Shake before use and apply liberally to your body. (It's a good idea to do a patch test first on a small area, such as your wrist, to make sure you aren't sensitive to the citrus or the oils.) Enjoy!

Store the remainder in the refrigerator (or ice house) between uses.

Makes $1\frac{1}{3}$ cups

TAKE A SPONGE BATH

Imagine taking a weekly bath in a wooden tub, filled with water that's been heated on the stove or over the fire. Brrr. I came close to this scenario during one frigid winter. The water heater gave out, so Mom portaged boiling water into the tub for me. By the time she came back with another pan or kettle, the water had turned lukewarm, and I was shivering. Given this, it's strange that I still love baths so very much.

I don't think bath time was a favorite activity on the prairie. Gals had to be quick about it, seeing as they were scrubbing up in a tub and didn't have a lot of room in which to maneuver or a lot of privacy. When they took a bath once a week or, gasp, more infrequently, they had to wash up somehow, seeing as frontier living wasn't exactly clean. Wholesome, yes. Clean, not so much.

WHAT YOU WILL NEED

Bowl and pitcher
Soap (either bar or liquid)
Sponge or washcloth
Towel
Water

When you are too busy to stop and smell the bubble bath, at least freshen up your bits and pieces. Back in the day, well-to-do folks had a china pitcher and bowl. My parents had an antique set on their bureau in their bedroom. They kept spare change in it, but why not use it for its original purpose?

Fetch fresh water in the pitcher before you go to bed. In the morning, pour water into the bowl as necessary. Splash some water on your face. Add a dab of liquid soap on a sponge or washcloth, dip it in the water until it soaps up slightly, and squeeze out the excess water.

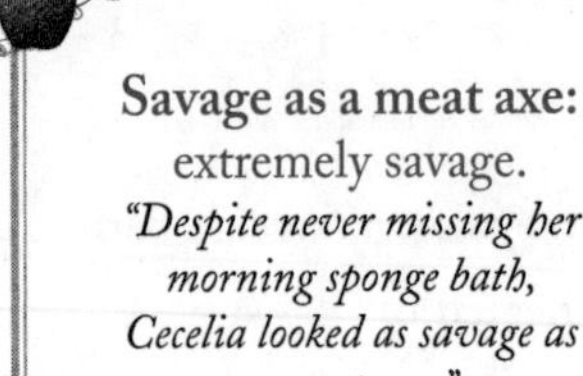

Savage as a meat axe: extremely savage. *"Despite never missing her morning sponge bath, Cecelia looked as savage as a meat axe."*

Now sponge your body, starting at your shoulders and working your way down. Periodically, rinse the sponge in the water bowl, squeeze out water, and repeat. When done, dispose of the used water. If you don't have a pitcher and bowl, use the sink. The important thing is to freshen the areas likely to carry dirt or body odor. Towel off, get dressed, and go. You've got to make hay while the sun shines!

CREATE A DRAWSTRING BAG

I was more than slightly obsessed with my mom's purse when I was growing up. It was filled with strange and wondrous things, from lipstick and cigarettes to pamphlets and pay stubs. Her wallet had cards of all sorts. I wanted a wallet badly. Somehow, those cards—all imprinted with her name—lent her an air of worth. The world knew she existed. She mattered.

Mom's purse was built for wear. To this day, she dumps all her change in the bottom of the bag, not bothering to throw it in a coin purse. When I was 10, it didn't seem a big deal to help myself to a buck or so of coins. These days, I am still fascinated with handbags, purses, shoulder bags, clutches, and the like. But they are my own and are not weighted down with coins. Like a good prairie gal, I know how valuable every penny is. To that end, here's a cute and economical way to make an adorable drawstring pouch (courtesy of my crafty chum Wendy Sloneker), perfect for gift giving, going out, or just tucking away a lip balm and spare change.

WHAT YOU WILL NEED

5 ½- by 14 ½-inch oblong piece of fabric (note that the sturdier the fabric, the sturdier the pouch)

Thread (cotton, polyester, or a cotton-poly blend)

Size 10 to 12 all-purpose sharp needle (this can depend on the type of fabric you are using)

Straight pins

2 feet ribbon or cord

When planning your pouch, think about what you want to use it for. If you want to make a rustic bag to hold marbles or jacks, consider cutting up an old flannel shirt and pairing it with a sturdy cord. If you want a delicate pouch to use as an evening bag or a sachet, choose a dreamy organza or silk with a satin or grosgrain ribbon. Or pick a no-fray fabric, such as Ultrasuede®, fleece, or felted items, for a nice, clean project. Use hem tape in lieu of pinning.

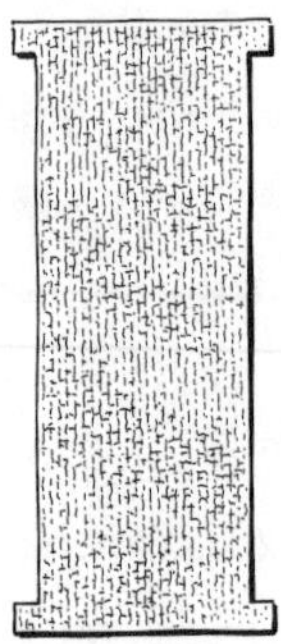

Lay out your fabric, right side up (the side you want to show when done). Cut the fabric so that each short end is ½ inch wider than the rest of the bag as shown in the illustration at left. Fold it in half. Pin the sides in place with a few straight pins—a straight pin every inch or so.

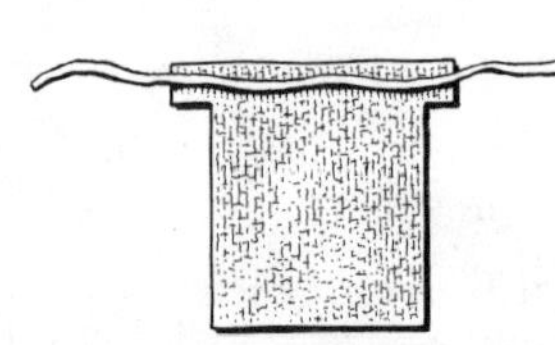

Thread your needle with about 2 feet of thread. Pull the thread through the needle and knot both ends together.

With the fabric inside out, sew up each side, starting at the bottom fold and working your way up. A **backstitch** will ensure that nothing falls out of your bag. Pass your needle through the two layers of fabric. Now poke the needle through the fabric about ½ inch away from the first stitch, and bring it up to the front of the piece. There should be a gap between your first stitch and where your needle is. Close the gap for a tight seam. Pass the needle down into the fabric right next to (or even into the actual hole of) your last stitch. Continue

All creation, all nature, all wrath: everything or everybody. *"Covered with bruises and grass stains, Jenny's mother said the horse pulled like all creation, as it dragged her across the field."*

in this manner until you reach the wider ends at the top edges.

Depending on how wide your ribbon or cord is, leave an unsewn top edge 2½ times the size of the ribbon. For instance, if your ribbon is ¼ inch wide, leave ⅝ inch of fabric at the top edge. Make sense?

Next, lay your ribbon across the unsewn top edge (see the bottom illustration on the facing page). Fold the top flap over the ribbon and pin the edge in place. At this point, gently pull the ribbon that peeks out on either side toward the top fold of your flap. This will ensure that you don't accidentally stitch the ribbon to the bag. Now sew the flap down across the top of your pouch, leaving each end of the flap open for the ribbon to move through. Repeat this process on the other side of

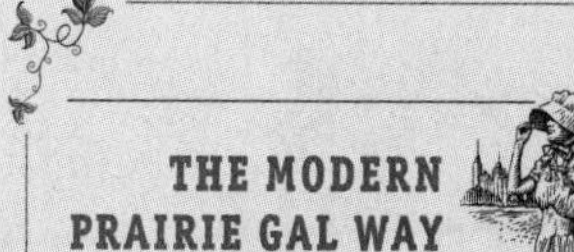

THE MODERN PRAIRIE GAL WAY

Back in the day, folks took baths once a week and it wasn't a cherished event. Pouring kettles of hot water into a metal tub in a cold kitchen isn't exactly the same experience as sinking into a bubbly bathtub in a candlelit bathroom. Sometimes they weren't able to take full baths and had to make do with cold sponge baths. These days, thank your lucky stars for the advancements in indoor plumbing and heating. Spend time luxuriating in a hot bath. Light a few votives (see p. 99 for instructions on making your own candles), pour your favorite potion into the tub, and turn on some music to soothe your soul. Close your eyes and think about all the honest work you did that day. Think about your elders and how their spirit paved the way for your life. Spend some time figuring out how to downsize your life so you can fill it back up with meaningful activities. Or just lie in the tub and count your blessings, one of which is a long, hot bath.

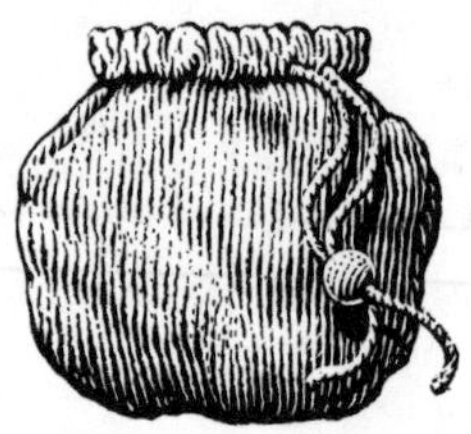

the pouch, sewing down the second flap of fabric and securing the ribbon inside the flap.

Turn inside out. You're almost there. You can fold in the edges of the pouch where the ribbon peeks through, or permanently tuck the raw edges out of sight with a few stitches.

Knot the ends of the ribbon together. You can even string both ends through one bead and knot the two ends together. This way, you can slide the bead up to secure the closure (see the illustration above).

TIP☞ *Using thread in a contrasting color, use a blanket or whipstitch to embellish the edges of the bag.*

- *Use different-colored strips for your flap to create a two-tone bag.*
- *Sew buttons onto your pouch in a random or pinwheel design.*
- *Embroider metallic thread through an organza pouch or embroidery floss through a thicker fabric.*
- *For a kid's bag, use cork or potatoes to create a stamp and decorate the bag with fabric paints.*
- *Cut up an old shirt strategically, so you end up having a pocket showing on the outside of your bag.*
- *Make a bag on a bigger scale and use it for a laundry bag or toy sack.*

STAYING CLEAN ON THE FRONTIER

Stains come in every shape and size, and pioneer women know all sorts of crafty methods of getting spots and smells out of fabric. These stain-fighting solutions come from Melissa Wagner, a true prairie girl in her own right and co-author of *Field Guide to Stains*.

Before you try removing a stain, there are a few general guidelines you should follow. If your garment was store-bought, there will be a label with manufacturer's instructions. If the item was hand-sewn, care is trickier. But no matter what you use to treat a stain, apply solutions to the back of the stain to push it out of the fabric, rather than into it. Treat the stain until it's gone, then leave it be. Never apply heat to the stain, as it will set. Air-dry items (the sun can also act as a mild bleaching agent) and treat again until the stain is gone.

A few tricky stains you might find on your person if you happen to be on the prairie (or at least outdoors):

Grass: Scrub stain with baking powder and an old toothbrush (or sponge it with white vinegar). Let the area sit for several minutes. Rinse and repeat as needed.

Sweat: Use white vinegar or ammonia and sponge the stained area. Repeat until the stain is removed or no more can be removed.

Berries: Berry stains should be treated immediately. If you are away from the homestead and can't take care of the stain right away, sprinkle

it with salt. Rinse the stain with cold water. Pour a dollop of liquid detergent on the stain (using bar or natural soap will set the stain). Let the stain sit for several minutes, then thoroughly rinse the back of the stain in hot water, letting the water pass through the fabric.

If you didn't notice the stain, make a paste of three parts borax to one part water and spread onto the stain. Let it sit for 15 minutes and rinse.

GATHERINGS

SOAPMAKING PARTY

I love hosting project parties, where we all work on or acquire a craft while catching up. And sometimes I like to experiment with a new skill while surrounded by equally curious crafters. For a fun party, try making soap.

Find a good basic recipe (see p. 67 or check out a book or website devoted to the art of soapmaking) and gather your soapmaking materials and ingredients. Instruct your guests to bring goggles, rubber gloves, long-sleeved clothing, and a mold for their soap, such as an ice tray.

When setting up your workspace, take pains to protect surfaces and rugs. Lay down plastic if need be. Put food and beverages far away from the workspace. Lye is not to be trifled with.

Purchase several essential oils for guests to add to their soap mixture. A few popular additions include:

* PEPPERMINT: A natural mental stimulant when inhaled, and the oil can cool and soothe upon contact.

* Lavender: Lavender smells lovely and ladylike but also relaxes and soothes the spirit. It is thought to promote a restful sleep, which is much needed after a day of industrious pursuits.

* Rosemary: This multipurpose oil can help dandruff, acne, and oily skin, and the popular herb smells invigorating.

* Grapefruit: Citrus is a natural pick-me-up, and grapefruit oil can help balance oily skin, in addition to treating stress and depression.

* Rose: This essential oil is wonderful for older skin, and the genteel smell lifts the spirits.

Based on the recipe on p. 67, add 1 to 2 teaspoons of essential oils to the soap mixture. When starting out, I'd recommend mixing no more than two oils together, as the scent and oil properties can compete with each other. And, just to be on the safe side, pregnant women (along with kids and pets) should probably steer clear of the activity altogether.

Serve drinks with straws so gloved hands can be kept away from beverages. Wash up thoroughly before bringing out snacks. Consider serving a few things in molds (but never reuse your soap molds for food): JELL-O and flavored ice cubes in whimsical ice trays, cupcakes in shaped tins. More prairie fare would include mason jars filled with sticks of beef jerky and peppermint sticks, bowls of popcorn balls (see p. 47), and pitchers of ice-cold lemonade.

It's always nice to give your guests a party favor. In this case, consider a fun mold or pretty packaging for their soap. Colored waxed papers and cellophanes, glassine envelopes, grosgrain ribbon, and rickrack trim can create rustic wrappings for handcrafted soaps.

All-overish: uncomfortable.

"Carrie noticed Robert looking at her during the church service and felt all-overish, but not necessarily in a bad way."

THE BEDROOM

In a world of sleek but bland furniture, I instead gravitate toward comforting quilts, knotty pine, and soft candlelight. I created a prairie haven in my bedroom to escape from my harried life—the last thing I want in my bedroom is anything that smacks of the newfangled. I get enough of that during my waking hours.

As a kid in the '70s, I regarded my bedroom as my sanctuary. Closing the door, I created a private world, where I could sing, dance, read, and dream. Like many prairie gals, I was often cold under the covers in the winter, so I invited our dog, Tippy, to act as a heat source and body pillow. She was happy to oblige. And in the summer, I slept with one leg slung over the covers to keep cool.

These days, my big-boned cat, Mac Daddy, fills the job of bed warmer admirably, curling up on an afghan I knitted or a quilt that my great-grandmother crafted. A woman's bedroom should be, in the words of Virginia Woolf, "a room of one's own," and there are countless ways to customize your own prairie-chic haven. I offer a few of my favorites here.

MIX LAVENDER LINEN WATERS

Just because deodorant and central air conditioning can sometimes be lacking on the plains doesn't mean that a pioneer woman has to surrender her toilette. Spritz your muslins and poplins with lavender-scented linen water before pressing and you'll be sure to turn heads and noses at the town's ice cream social or harness races. With all this attention, just remember to keep your cool no matter how hot it may get.

WHAT YOU WILL NEED

Sealed jar or container

2 teaspoons lavender essential oil

5 tablespoons 100-proof vodka

1 cup distilled water

Spray bottle

Combine the lavender oil and vodka and shake vigorously. Add the distilled water and pour into a spray bottle (glass is preferable). Shake gently before using. To use, mist on clothes before ironing your linens. Use it on your Sunday best, petticoats, work clothes, whatever and whenever you want to smell crisp and fresh. Heck, spray it on your curtains before pressing.

Yields approximately 1½ cups

BRAID A RAG RUG

In a world of Pottery Barns® and Crate and Barrels®, I'm constantly upgrading my home with new bits of furniture, shelving, and crockery. But I have no desire to swap out my rugs for sisal, tufted wool, or any sort of fancy floor coverings. I'm content to putter around my home, my feet warmed by the cheery oval rag rug my grandmother made so many years ago.

Grandma's bedroom closet was filled with hat boxes, which were often stuffed with treasures other than hats. One drawer contained old greeting cards, another jewelry. Plastic beaded necklaces were thrown in a drawer together, creating a colorful jumble. Delicate earrings and a stylish pony pin, both crafted from Mexican silver, were hidden away in boxes, and large flower pins dotted her dressing table.

Stuffed in a large plastic bag next to Grandma's bed were rags, strips of fabric she used for quilts and rugs. She used anything—worn-out work shirts, bedsheets, fabric she picked up at a rummage sale. She was always industrious. Back when my family raised chickens and other livestock, she'd go to the feed store to pick out feed

> **Hornswoggle, honey-fuggled:** to cheat; to pull the wool over one's eyes.
> *"Minnie was nearly hornswoggled by a merchant when she tried to buy muslin in town."*

WHAT YOU WILL NEED

Old, clean garments and fabrics

Scissors

Straight pins

Quilting thread
(available in fabric and craft stores)

Heavy-duty needle
(a semicircular needle is helpful but not necessary)

bags made out of a printed cloth and make dresses out of them, throwing any remnants into the scrap bag. Like my grandmother, I hate throwing things away, especially clothes that seemed like a good idea at the time, so here's how to recycle that pink neon camp shirt from 1987 and turn it into your very own rag rug.

Gather worn clothes and fabric. Most anything will do, except for heavy fabrics like denim and thick wool. Make sure all fabric is clean. Cut off fastenings, such as buttons and zippers, and trim off pockets and the like. Cut out seams and hems; the goal is to end up with large, flat pieces of fabric.

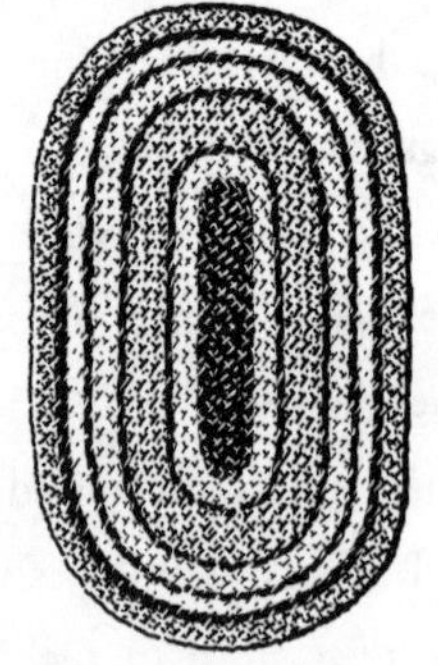

Next, cut your cloth into 3-inch-wide strips, the longer the better. With a needle and thread, sew the short ends of the fabrics together to create long strips. Mix and match colors and patterns for a rustic rug.

The long (length) edges of your strips will be frayed. You don't want that to peek out of your braided rug, so fold the edges under about ¼ of an inch. Then fold the strip in half lengthwise, pinning in place every so often to keep the strips folded, with edges tucked inside out of sight. (If you have nimble fingers, you can also try to just tuck the edges in with your thumbs as you braid.)

Once you have three long, sewn-together, folded and pinned strips, it's time to braid. Knot the ends of the three strips together and loop them over a doorknob. (You'll trim the knotted end later.) Keep the strips taut and start braiding, just as you would hair (see p. 58). Make sure you remove the straight pins as you go.

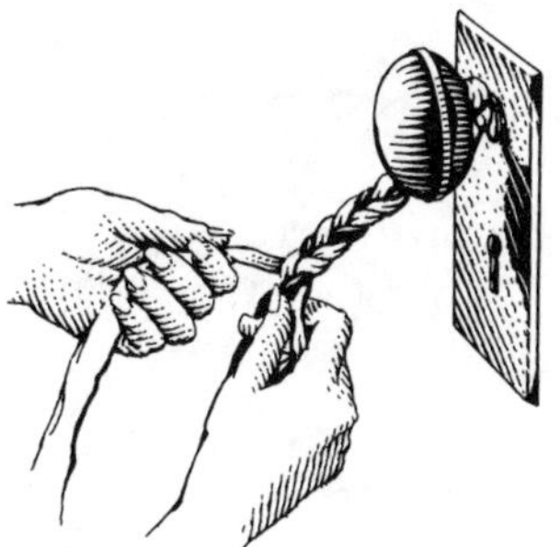

When you come to the end of a strip, sew on a new length and continue to braid. When you have a good length of braid, you can start coiling your rug on a table or flat surface. For an oval rug, lay 12 inches of braid on a table and then coil the rest of the braid around it, pinning the braids to each other loosely with straight pins. For a round rug, just start coiling and pinning the braid around itself so that it spirals into an ever-expanding circle.

Using doubled quilting thread threaded through a sturdy needle, sew the braids to each other with the trusty whipstitch. To whipstitch, pull the thread through the inside braid from top to bottom, leaving about a 6- to 10-inch tail (that will be woven in later), then pull it up from the bottom to the top of the braid that butts up against it. Continue in this manner, looping or "whipping" your thread down through one braid loop and then up through the other. As you do this, work to keep the rug flat. When stitching together a sharp turn on an oval rug, the stitches on the inner braid should be closer together than the stitches on the outer braid in order to make the turn smoothly.

When the rug reaches your desired size, cut the last strips so they are narrower and braid them so the braid gradually comes to a point that will be easy to sew down and hide. Trim the ends, as well as any ends from the center that may be lurking about, such as the excess you used to hang your braid from the doorknob.

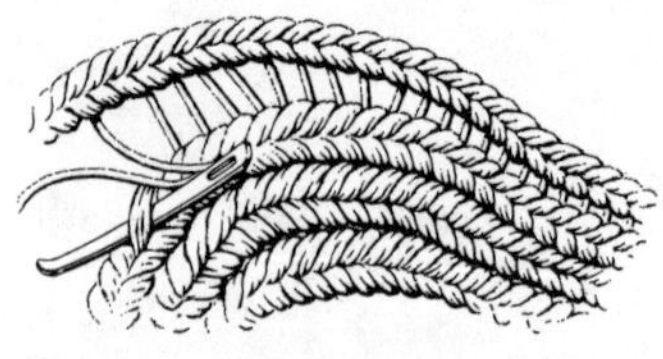

Place your rug in a place where family and friends can fully appreciate it.

MAKE AND USE RAG CURLERS

My mom had all sorts of mysterious tools and unguents tucked away in the linen closet. I pulled out her basket of gray, bristly curlers one

evening and decided to turn my ordinary hair into the bouncy, curly locks of *Seventeen* models.

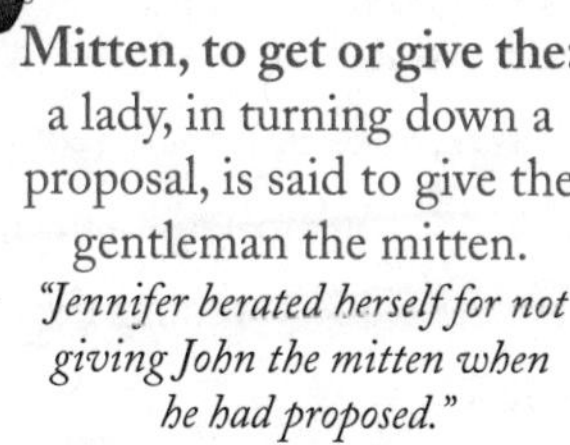
Mitten, to get or give the: a lady, in turning down a proposal, is said to give the gentleman the mitten. *"Jennifer berated herself for not giving John the mitten when he had proposed."*

That night, with prickly curlers pulling my hair tight, I didn't sleep a wink. With all the modern advances made in technology, science, and medicine, you'd think that curlers would have advanced beyond crude torture devices. Prairie girls, however, were ahead of their time. They dreamed the night away, their hair tucked under sleep caps, curling gently with the help of rag curlers.

While rags were often tied into hair after a Saturday night bath so curls would be fresh for church on Sunday, you can try them out and tie them on any day of the week. These simple instructions are courtesy of Peri Coleman, a modern-day prairie girl.

WHAT YOU WILL NEED

Hair clip or hairpins

"Rags," 25 to 30 strips of cotton flannel, 1 to 2 inches wide and 8 to 12 inches long

Damp hair, at least shoulder length

For rag curlers, shoulder-length or longer hair works best. Wash, towel-dry, and comb your hair. You want to roll your rag curlers, starting with the bottom layers of your hair and moving to the crown. To that end, grab a hair clip or hairpins and loosely twist your top layers of hair up and out of the way, leaving only the bottom 1-inch layer of hair. Starting at the nape of your neck and working forward toward your face, take a 1-inch section of hair. Slip the rag under the section, hold it against the end of the lock, and roll the hair down and under the cloth, trapping the rag in the middle of the coil. When the hair reaches the scalp, tie a snug square knot (as my mother says, tie right over left and then left over right). Finish the bottom layer of hair and then take down another 1-inch-thick layer, pinning up the top hair. Work from the back to the front in the same manner. Continue until you have wrapped all of your hair.

Wash your face, brush your teeth, and climb under the coverlet. In the morning, contain your excitement as you rush to the mirror. Untie each knot, starting with the bottom layer and working up. Gently loosen each coil, and when all the flannel strips have been removed, gently finger-comb your hair to loosen up your curls. Tie back with a ribbon if you want to look your Sunday best. Leave your curls loose and messy if you're planning to hit the saloon instead.

DARN A SOCK

I learned to knit about 10 years ago and never looked back. And some of the most satisfying garments to create are socks. The care that goes into knitting a pair of socks is evident in the turned and reinforced heel and the special pattern on the cuff. So whether the sock was purchased at the town mercantile or lovingly knitted by hand, I don't throw away a great pair of socks when a toe or heel pokes through. I darn them (a fancy way of saying that I mend the hole), which is as easy as it is satisfying.

WHAT YOU WILL NEED

Light bulb or hard rubber ball

Thread, embroidery floss, or machine-washable sock yarn

Needle appropriate to your darning material (straight needle for thread, tapestry needle for yarn)

Place a light bulb or rubber ball into the sock and push it against the hole so that it becomes taut. Trim off the loose strands around the hole.

Thread a needle with your darning strand of choice (most people choose a color that matches their sock but you could also mend your sock with a colorful contrasting thread for fun). You'll need about 2 feet of thread for small holes. Do not knot the ends together; instead, pull only about 6 inches of your thread through the needle eye and leave the other end long.

Basically, you are going to weave a patch of thread over the hole. First, secure the edges of the hole by whipstitching around the entire hole. To whipstitch, bring your thread through the sock fabric, very close to the hole, from the inside of the sock to the outside. Leave about 6 to 8 inches of thread sticking out. You'll weave the ends in later. Loop your thread around the edge of the hole and poke the needle through the inside of the sock close to where you made your first stitch. Continue in this manner around the hole, looping or "whipping" your thread around the edge of the hole. You're creating a sturdy edge around your hole. Check your thread. If you're running low, leave a tail of 6 inches on your whipstitched handiwork to weave in later, and restring your needle with fresh thread.

Now starting at the top of the hole and stitching into your new whipstitched edge, stitch horizontally across the hole from left to right and then back again, right to left. Continue stitching back and forth across the hole from top to bottom. The threads will start to look like they are on a loom.

When you reach the bottom of the hole, repeat the process vertically, this time left to right. Weave your working thread in and out of the horizontal threads. Sew up and down across the hole, weaving in and out of the horizontal threads and making the patch as tight as possible. When you get to the opposite side of the hole, weave the ends of your thread into the sock. Remove the rubber ball or light bulb. Wash the sock so the patch becomes more pliable and fabriclike.

QUILT A SAMPLER

I am a bit obsessed with quilts. There, I'll admit it. As soon as I developed some taste—which was at around age 14—I spread a handmade quilt over my bed. I've never looked back. I can't afford to collect quilts but even so, I have three—two from my great-grandmother and one from my grandmother—carefully draped over a door and on the back of a chair and at the foot of my bed. They are worn in places, but they provide me with more warmth than any of my other belongings.

My good friend Susie Stevenson is my longtime craft buddy. I've followed her around to quilting expos so I could pet the amazing masterpieces on display and marvel at the many gorgeous squares of fabric. Susie was kind enough to make me a quilted pillow that now sits on the chair along with my grandmother's quilt. So naturally I turned to Susie when I wanted to make something—in this case, a nine-square sampler—out of all those "fat quarters" I have accumulated.

WHAT YOU WILL NEED

9 pieces of cotton fabric, cut into 3½-inch squares, washed and pressed

Sharp hand needle (any sort of sewing needle is fine, as long as you can thread it)

100-percent cotton sewing thread, color of your choice

Thimble

11½-inch square of quilt batting (or you can use a clean piece of flannel or blanket)

11½-inch square of light-colored cotton backing fabric

Tape

9 safety pins

100-percent cotton quilting thread, color of your choice

Handful of straight pins

Preparing the Fabric

You are creating an heirloom, so choose all-cotton fabrics and thread. Polyester thread and fabrics wear differently than cotton and, after 100 years, may look oddly bright against your cotton pieces.

You are going to make a nine-square sampler. To do this, you will sew three rows of three squares together on the front of your sampler (to create a larger square) and a neutral piece of fabric to back your design (muslin is a great choice).

Keeping this in mind, select a combination of light and dark fabrics so they contrast when placed next to each other. Think of a checkerboard or a tic-tac-toe grid. For the top row, you might place dark/light/dark squares next to each other. The center row would have light/dark/light. The third and bottom row would have dark/light/dark. Make sense?

Choose five squares of the same dark fabric and four squares of the same light fabric, or you could choose five different fabrics and

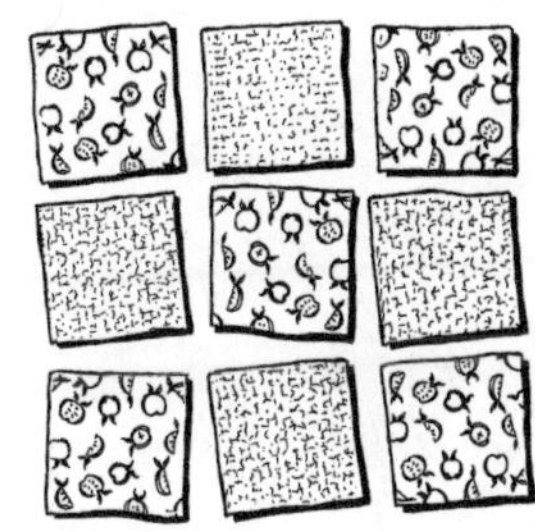

patterns with the same color value (i.e., dark) and four different light fabrics. This works great for scraps. If you are using cut-up clothing, choose cotton fabrics and press them before using.

Once you have the fabrics for the front of your sampler, cut them into 3½-inch squares. This will give you 3-inch squares with a ¼-inch seam allowance on all sides.

For backing, cut a muslin or cotton fabric into an 11½-inch square.

TIP *If you want to hang your quilt, sew small loops of fabric onto the backing. You can run a small rod or pole through the loops and then hang it, or you can use nails or push pins on the loops to secure your work to a wall.*

Piecing the Nine-Square

On a flat surface, arrange your nine pieces how you want them to appear. Thread a needle with 2 feet of cotton sewing thread, knotting one end (or forgoing a knot altogether). With a pencil, lightly draw a line ¼ inch from each edge on the wrong side of the light squares. You are now ready to sew.

Pick up the top left and top center pieces, and sew them together using a running stitch (see the illustration on p. 96), as small and even as you can. A running stitch is super easy: Go up and down through

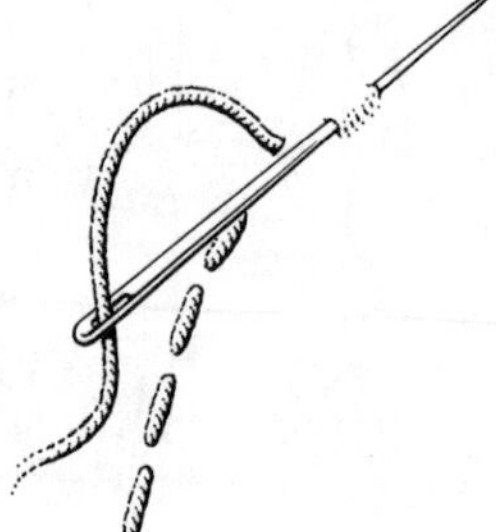

the fabric and, in this case, accumulate several stitches on your needle before you draw the needle and thread through the cloth (it saves time).

You want to sew the pieces with a straight ¼-inch seam, so pin the pieces together if necessary. Pick up the top right piece and sew it to the center piece, on the opposite side of the top right piece (you are creating a strip three squares long). Sew the middle and bottom rows in the same fashion.

Press the seams on the back of each strip. A rule of thumb is to press toward the dark pieces so that when you sew all the strips together, the seams dovetail with each other. Using a small running stitch, sew the three rows together, again using a ¼-inch seam allowance (draw a light pencil line on the wrong side of one strip). You have pieced a nine-patch quilt block by hand. Doesn't it look charming?

Assembling Your Sampler

Now it's time for a backing. Your muslin backing should be at least 1 inch larger than the block (9½ by 9½ inches) on all sides, which in this case would make the backing 11½ by 11½ inches.

Cut out batting (you can use quilt batting or even an old blanket or piece of flannel cut to 11½ by 11½ inches). Place the backing on a flat surface, wrong side up, and tape it down so it's flat but not stretched out. Place your batting on top of this, then place your quilt block face up on top. You have created a batting sandwich of sorts. Now, using safety pins, pin through the center of each square, and through all three layers. Remove the tape.

Quilting Your Work

To turn your nine-patch block into a real quilted piece, you have to stitch through all three layers in a free-form or structured design. Switching to hand-quilting thread (which is thicker than sewing thread) and using your trusty running stitch again, follow the seams, or quilt ¼ inch in from the seams for echo squares. You can stitch Xs and Os, flowers, curvy lines, whatever you fancy. For a more structured design, trace around a template,

THE MODERN PRAIRIE GAL WAY

Sometimes it wasn't possible to make the long trek into town for a quilting bee. But women remained ever industrious, dipping into a bag of scraps, old clothes, and rags. When a prairie gal got hitched, she packed up the precious quilt and other hand-worked linens she had made over the years and carefully put away for her future. From an early age, a prairie gal was proficient both in quiltmaking and keeping an eye on her future. And as she set up house with her new husband, she would spread her quilt over their bed, both lending her a touch of home and comforting her about her new married life. That's the power of an heirloom, even one you create yourself. Since piecework is so portable, start creating your heirloom quilt with nine squares (see p. 93). In no time, you'll have enough for a full-on quilt for you or a loved one to cherish.

marking your work temporarily with soap or dressmaker's chalk. The important thing is to stitch through all three layers with small stitches to create a quilted effect.

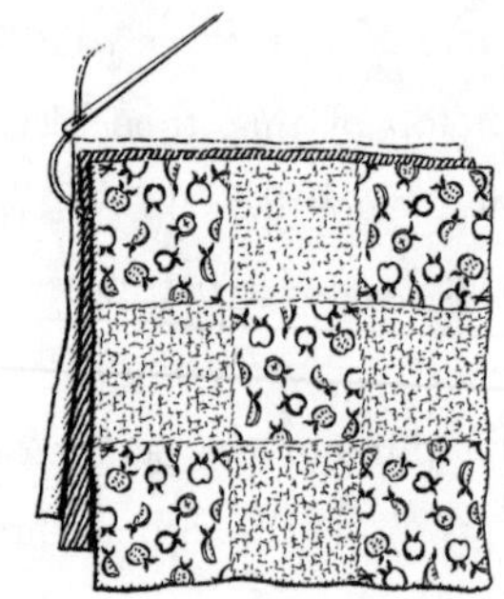

Binding the Edges

Let's get rid of all the raw edges. Fold the backing—you should have an extra inch all around—over the front of your work. Tuck the raw edges under, and pin the backing down all the way around your sampler on the right side using straight pins. Pin the corners so they come to a point. To do this, sew one edge all the way to the corner. When you turn the corner to sew along the adjoining side, fold the corner over the previous sewn-down edge so it's flush and at a 90-degree angle. Examine your pinning to ensure that the edging looks even all the way around. All four sides should have the same allowance. Using a small, even stitch, sew through the nine-patch—not the batting or backing layer—to secure. You do not want these stitches to show through to the back. Continue to sew all the way around, knotting and securing your thread. That's it!

TIP *Label your work. It may not seem like it now, but you are creating an heirloom. Let future generations know at whose hands this work was wrought.*

CANDLEMAKING

Candles are a regular indulgence for me, but on the prairie they were absolutely necessary. While people often were snug in bed by 8 o'clock, there were reasons they needed to see after dark. Prairie men may have preferred to check on the livestock with a kerosene lamp, but it was usually by candlelight that prairie gals finished up their needlework or read stories in *The Youth's Companion* or in *Godey's Lady's Book.*

Now, I light candles nearly every night. They are comforting, they smell great, and they provide a relaxing atmosphere for winding down after a long day. I often spend hard-earned cash on a pillar, taper, or votive, wooed by the smell of lemongrass, sage, currant, grapefruit, basil, mandarin, lavender, and even leather.

WHAT YOU WILL NEED

Double boiler

Candy thermometer

Mold release spray, such as PAM® (optional)

2 pounds wax suitable for votives (paraffin wax bricks or even candle stubs)

1 tablespoon essential or fragrance oil(s) of your choice (optional)

10 pretabbed wicks (3 inches long) suitable for votives

10 metal votive molds

The materials can all be found at a craft store, candle-supply store, or grocery store. To keep things from getting messy, cover your working surface with several layers of newspaper before you begin.

The first step is to melt your wax safely. To do this, bring a half-filled pot of water to a rolling boil and then turn it to medium-high. Place a double boiler in the pot, making sure that no water overflows. If it does, pour out enough water so the double boiler can sit comfortably in the pot. Clip a candy thermometer to the inside of the double boiler. If you don't have a double boiler, use a smaller pot or glass measuring bowl in a larger pot of boiling water.

Add wax. When melting wax, a good target temperature for votives is 175°F (although check the packaging of the wax you purchase, as it may list a different melt temperature). Keep a close eye on the temperature as the wax melts; it can become dangerous when it reaches its "flash point," around 300°F.

Meanwhile, lightly coat your molds with a silicone spray or a PAM-type cooking spray to help remove the candles from the molds after they cool.

When your wax reaches 175°F and is thoroughly melted, remove the double boiler from heat, add your essential oil(s) of choice (I love lavender and rosemary), and carefully pour the wax up to the lip of each votive mold. Save about ⅕ of your wax to top off your candles after they start to cool (they will create a depression in the middle of the candle, like a fallen soufflé).

While the wax is cooling, prep your pretabbed wicks. Tug a bit to straighten them, then insert a wick into each mold. The tab on the wick's end should stick to the bottom, so try to position it in the center of each mold. Once affixed to the bottom, pull gently on the wick to straighten it out. The wax needs to cool for several hours, at which point you should see a depression in the middle of each candle. Heat up and melt down the remaining wax. When the wax reaches 190°F, fill the dents in your candle so it is topped off (avoid pouring so that it overflows, however). Allow your candles to cool again. Remove them from the molds. If they don't want to come out of their molds, stick them in a freezer for 10 minutes and try again.

Always burn votives in a votive holder. If you burn them without a holder, they will liquefy and create a big melted mess. The typical votive will burn for approximately 15 hours.

Yields 10 votive candles

THE MODERN PRAIRIE GAL WAY

During long winters, prairie folk had it hard. Food was scarce, wood often nonexistent, and kerosene expensive as it became more limited in supply. So they used their wits and anything around them to start and keep a fire crackling. Instead of kerosene, resourceful women smeared axle grease onto scraps of fabric tied around an old button for makeshift "button lamps." These days, things don't usually get so extreme. When the weather dips below freezing, we just turn up the thermostat. But if you are exposed to fierce weather or simply want to make a fire, think about all the items you have in your possession that could be used as a fire starter, as long as you have a match or lighter: lipsticks, petroleum jelly, hand sanitizer, perfume. Anything containing alcohol can potentially be used to stoke a fire. Just make sure you've got tinder, kindling, and wood to keep the home fires burning.

EMBROIDER A PILLOWCASE

Every self-respecting pioneer girl knows she must master embroidery; after all, she has to embellish linens and lace for her hope chest. It's never too early to start planning for your future home or decorating your current homestead. Embroidery is portable and relatively easy, and it's a cheap way to decorate your linens and your clothing, with a down-home brand of chic.

Sit near a window on a quiet, sunny afternoon, bend over your embroidery hoop, and channel that frontier woman who diligently worked to make everything around her beautiful. For sweet dreams, embroider your pillowcases with of wagon wheels or sprightly green beans. (I borrow these designs and techniques from embroidery instructor and graphic designer Alicia Freile, who designs and embroiders her own line of handbags [www.gauchita.com].)

WHAT YOU WILL NEED

Size 18 to 22 embroidery needle (any size needle will do, as long as you can thread embroidery floss through it and pass it through your pillowcase fabric)

Cotton embroidery floss (I suggest DMC® six-strand embroidery floss in colors 420 and 422 for the wagon wheel and 3850 and 3851 for the green beans)

4- or 7-inch embroidery hoop

Small pair of sharp scissors

White cotton pillowcases (pass your needle through the fabric before beginning to make sure that the weave is not too tight)

Dressmaker's carbon paper with pencil, or transfer pencil

Unless you're able to embroider free-form, you will need a pattern to follow. You can draw a rough outline of a design onto your cloth with chalk or pencil, or you can trace a pattern onto it with carbon paper, much like a seamstress would do when transferring a pattern onto fabric. You can always buy iron-on transfers, but I've supplied a couple of prairie-worthy design inspirations. Here's how to get a design onto fabric.

You'll need carbon paper, the kind used for patternmaking (available at craft and fabric stores). Trace the image onto the fabric by slipping the paper, face down, between the design and the back of the fabric.

Another option is to use a transfer pencil. Using the illustrations in this book as inspiration, draw a wagon wheel or string bean to create a template. Trace over your design template with the transfer pencil (note that this won't work with lettering, as the design will be reversed on the fabric when transferred). With the design face up, place the back of the fabric on top of the design on a flat surface and lightly iron. The design should be transferred onto the fabric.

Now it's time to make your fabric taut. Separate the two embroidery hoops from each other. Lay your fabric so your design is within the inner, nonadjustable hoop. Place the adjustable hoop over and around these, and press down. Make sure the top hoop is not too tight, or you may tear the fabric. Pull your fabric taut like a drum, and tighten the hoop's screw. Retighten and readjust the fabric and hoop as needed as you embroider. Whenever you put down your work for any long periods of time, loosen the screws and let your embroidery breathe.

Patience was an applied virtue on the frontier, but it is harder to achieve and maintain in these modern times. Take a breath, make a pot of tea, and begin to embroider.

Cut a piece of embroidery floss about 12 inches long (if you use a really long strand for the whole design, your floss can become tangled or simply unwieldy) and thread it through your needle. Pull a few inches through (enough so that your floss won't come off the needle while you're working), and make a knot an inch or two from the longer end.

Starting from the back of your fabric (which should feature your design tracing), bring your needle through the fabric from back to front and pull the floss through until the knot touches the fabric. Pass the needle back through the fabric, staying on the tracing. Hurray! You've just embroidered your first stitch!

It may not look like much, but your artistry will quickly be revealed as your design takes shape. There are two main stitches you need in your crafty arsenal, and you can use either to create your rolling wagon wheel or snappy green bean design.

The basic stitch is called a **backstitch** (see the top illustration on the facing page). The embroidered piece will look as if you have laid each stitch end to end. It's called a backstitch because you are embroidering backward. Let me explain.

To make this tidy and speedy stitch, pick up your needle. Remember you've just made one stitch and your needle should be on the underside of your fabric. Following the tracing, poke the needle through

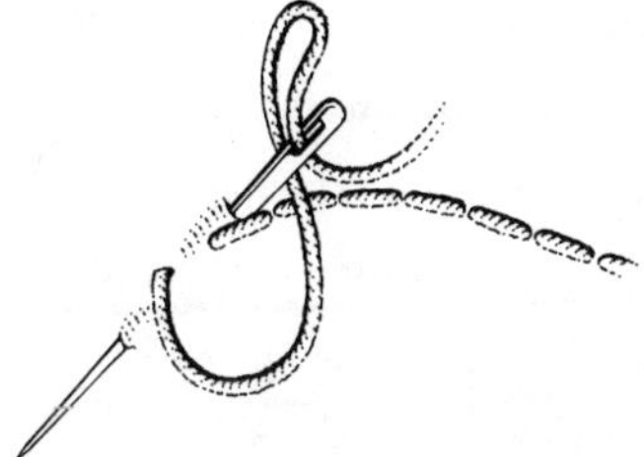

the fabric about a ½ inch away from the first stitch and bring it up to the front of the piece. There should be a gap between your first stitch and where your needle is. You need to close the gap to create a seamless line to your design. Pass the needle down into the fabric right next to (or even into the actual hole of) your last stitch. See? You have a continuous line of embroidery floss. Continue in this manner until you reach the end of your design or you run out of floss.

A **split stitch** (see the illustration below) works in a similar way but you take it even further. I like using split stitches because it creates more of a three-dimensional texture to the design and makes the tracing look lush and full. To create a split stitch, you will be "splitting" the floss with your needle. Your floss is made of several strands (or plies). If using a six-strand embroidery floss, you will want to pass your needle between the six plies, with three on each side.

Okay, so you've made your first stitch and your needle is on the back of your fabric. Bring the needle up through the middle of the first stitch, so the needle divides the floss in two. Now make a short stitch (use your own judgment for what constitutes "short," usually ½ inch),

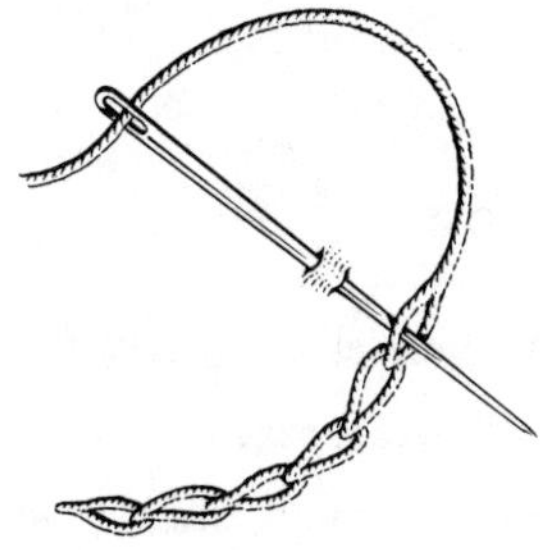

Any prairie lass worth her weight knew how to knit, sew, and embroider. She knitted mittens for Christmas gifts, added knitted edging to a skirt or petticoat, and kept warm with handmade mufflers and hats. Once you've got the hang of knitting, consider adding a knitted trim to a skirt, or knitting up a flower and pinning it to your lapel, prairie chic style. There are all sorts of ways to incorporate your handicrafts into your everyday accessorizing. And let's not forget about the pleasure and thriftiness of knitting gifts for others. In true frontier fashion, consider unraveling a sweater you don't particularly care for and reincarnate it in the form of a snug scarf.

bringing your needle down through the fabric, making sure that you are staying on your tracing. Continue in this fashion, splitting the previous stitch with each new one you make.

If you are about to run out of floss or reach the end of your design, leave a short tail for your first length of floss (on the back of your fabric, of course), then rethread your needle with a new piece of floss. Knot the loose strand as close to the fabric as you can. When you've completed your design, secure the stray strands: On the backside of the fabric, lay the loose strands over the line of your embroidery and whipstitch (see p. 87–88) around the loose embroidery floss and embroidered stitches, taking care not to pass the needle through the pillowcase fabric so it won't show on the front. When everything has been secured, weave the remaining thread back and forth through some of your stitches on the back of your fabric. Knot and trim the remaining floss.

Now that you have the tools to embellish just about anything, let's embroider some pillowcases and start filling your hope chest with lovely linens.

For wagon wheels

You can adorn your pillowcase with one or a whole string of wheels. Consider spacing them out evenly so you have an entire caravan of wagon wheels gracing your linens. And when your man tries to bring a wagon wheel coffee table into the house, you just tell him you're already full up.

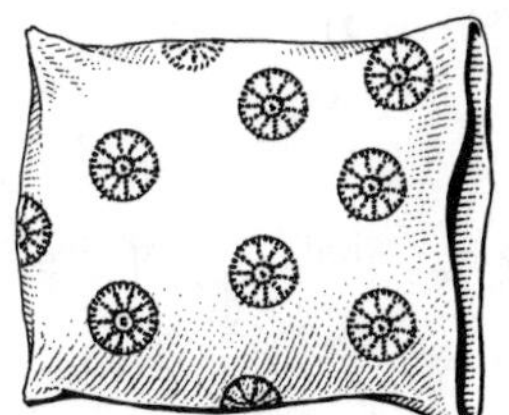

If you want an extra touch of color, add some blades of green grass along the bottom of the wheel. Giddyup!

For green beans

I like the idea of sprinkling various-size green beans all over pillowcases. Maybe you will dream of hunky farmers selling their wares at a county fair or outdoor market. Or just sparingly edge the pillowcase with one bean or two for an unexpected punch of color in your prairie pad.

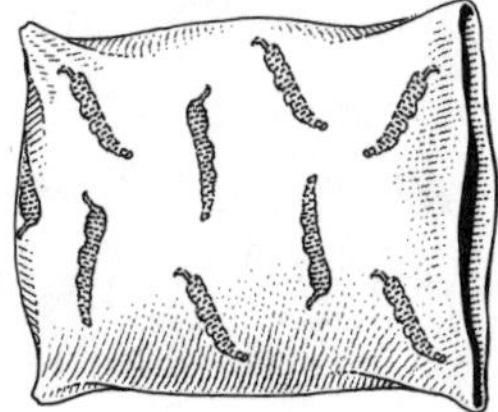

CONCOCT A NIGHT CREAM

My skin is smooth and creamy, if I do say so myself. It looks as if I've always worn a bonnet to guard against the effects of the harsh sun. The truth is, I've done a lot more than wear a hat at high noon. From a young age, I've worn sunscreen, I've cleansed, I've exfoliated, and I've moisturized. After a long stretch in the fields or in front of the computer, I like to give my skin an extra dose of moisture before retiring to my snug bunk. Here's how to whip up an especially delicious treat for your face.

WHAT YOU WILL NEED

Glass bowl or double-boiler

3 tablespoons sweet almond oil

2 tablespoons hydrous lanolin (lanolin that has been combined with purified water)

2 tablespoons cocoa butter

2 teaspoons rosewater (see p. 57 for instructions on making rosewater)

½ teaspoon honey

6 drops rose essential oil

If you have a double boiler, pull it out. (If you don't have one, a glass bowl can be used in its place.) Heat a pan of water over medium-high heat. When the water starts to boil, turn down the heat to medium. Place the double boiler in the water and add the sweet almond oil, hydrous lanolin, and cocoa butter. As the ingredients melt, stir with a metal spoon until completely blended.

Remove the double boiler from the heat, and let the mixture cool. Add the rosewater, honey, and rose essential oil, whisk until blended, and scoop into a sterilized plastic or glass jar (sterilize your jar by dipping it into a hot-water bath and letting it dry).

Before applying to your face, test out your night cream by rubbing a bit into your wrist. If you have no reaction other than supple skin, apply a dime-size dollop to a clean face before going to bed. Store in a cool place.

Yields 1/2 cup

LACE A CORSET

A proper young lady never went off the homestead without being properly laced up, comfort be damned. While wearing a corset these days is considered racy, it was the height of decorum and a necessary underpinning for decent, God-fearing women. Lacing yourself into a corset was a way to secure your sexuality and tuck it out of sight. Whatever your reason, slipping into a corset is a surefire way

> **Inexpressibles:** euphemism for pants or trousers.
> *"Penny secretly longed to wear inexpressibles rather than her corset when playing in the schoolyard."*

to give your shape, well, *shape*. And just like a prairie lass, you'll have your corset secreted away beneath your various layers...or then again, maybe you'll choose to display your assets to their best advantage.

WHAT YOU WILL NEED

Corset

Patience

Another person,
at least for initial fitting

The first thing to do is lace the corset, the tighter the better. You don't have to hold on to a bedpost while a servant huffs and puffs until you reach an 18-inch waist. However, with well-secured laces, you can create an hourglass figure without doing any permanent damage to your internal organs.

If you have hooks in front instead of just laces, secure the middle hook and work up and down from there. Then work to tighten the laces that are in back. There are usually two sets of laces on a corset—laces that crisscross from the top of the corset to the waistline and laces that start at the bottom of the corset and end at the waistline.

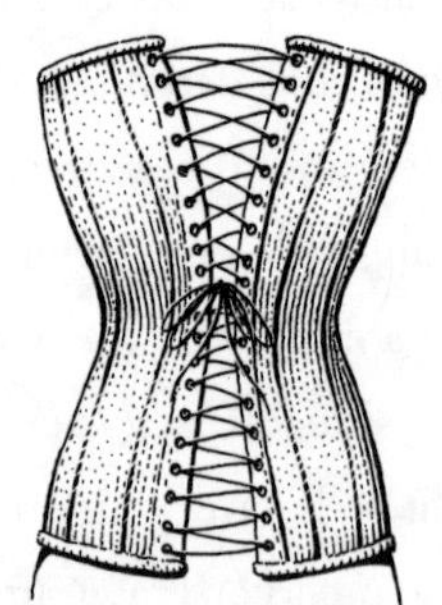

Ask a girlfriend to help with the initial fitting. If you go it alone, you may have to take your corset on and off while you adjust it. Work from the bodice toward the waistline, putting your index finger under each X and pulling the Xs snugly as you go. When you reach the waist, tie the ends of the laces together temporarily. Now work your way from the bottom of the corset up to the waist, pulling Xs in the same manner. Does the corset feel snug but not uncomfortable? Perfect! Tie all four laces together in a bow and admire your womanly form.

Don't lace too tightly at first. Your corset should feel tight but not to the point where you can't breathe. After a few days you can pull in the stays just a wee bit more. At first, you'll also find that you have to do certain things differently—bending, sitting, turning—so wear the corset every day for a few hours at a time until you get the hang of moving around. And remember to drink lots of fluids and eat—prairie women do not faint.

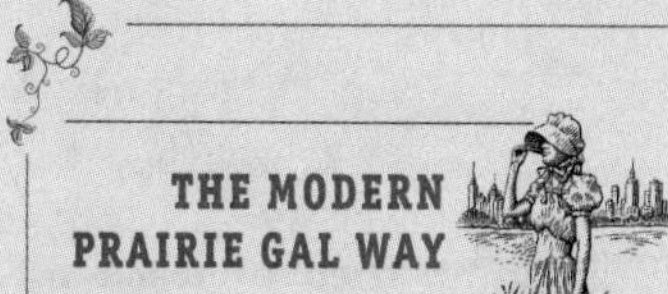

THE MODERN PRAIRIE GAL WAY

When it came to corsets, many prairie tomboys tried to go without proper underpinnings, much to their mothers' dismay. After all, it does restrict your movement when you're trying to play in the schoolyard with the boys. But as soon as a young girl took a shine to one of those neighboring farm boys, she became interested in looking more grown-up. Since she didn't have the opportunity to go to the mall for a sophisticated makeover, she had to explore other acceptable means of looking like a lady. That meant strapping herself into a corset that made her figure adopt a comely hourglass shape. The boys found such a figure fetching back then and they still do. Today, to get the same effect but minus the corset, sport shapely jackets and curve-hugging skirts to best show off your form.

KNIT A SHAWL

My grandma tried to teach me to knit, crochet, and sew, without much success. When I tried to crochet—with a god-awful yarn variegated in baby blue, pink, and white that I thought was the bee's knees—all I could manage to do was create a really long chain. I never quite figured out how to turn my work and go the other way.

I started knitting as an adult and finally took to it like a fish to water or a prairie gal to a homespun skill. Since then, I've taught several gals how to knit during cozy knitting circles. While I've provided the basic instruction to make a rustic shawl for cozy nights in a cold landscape, try gathering up some fellow prairie gals and having a knitting circle of your own. You'll learn a new craft and get the news from the neighboring farm at the same time.

> **Full chisel:**
> at full speed; executed with everything you've got.
> *"Grace went full chisel knitting her shawl so she could finish it in time for Christmas."*

The Cast-On

Getting stitches on a needle is called "casting on." While there are several ways to do it, I'm going to show you the cable cast-on. The good thing about this pattern is that you only need to cast on two stitches.

Leaving a long tail (here, about 10 inches), make a slipknot and place it on a needle. To make a slipknot, lay your yarn tail on a flat surface and make a loop near where the tail becomes your ball of yarn. Place the tail of yarn under the loop, then place a knitting needle under the bar of yarn within the loop you just made with the tail. Pull both ends of the yarn to complete the slipknot. You've made your first stitch.

Hold the needle with the stitch in your left hand. With the other needle in your right hand, insert the tip into the stitch (from front to back and under the left needle). Now grab the working yarn (not the tail) with the tip, and pull it through the first stitch, creating a loop (see the illustration above). Place that loop onto the tip of the left-hand needle. You've magically got two stitches!

Repeat the same process until you have the number of stitches on the needle that your pattern specifies. For this shawl, you only need these first two.

The Knit Stitch

With just two stitches—the knit and the purl—you can knit virtually anything. But even with just the humble knit stitch, you can create all sorts of garments. This shawl is knitted through the use of **garter**

stitch (knitting every row) and **yarnover increases**, which create a lacy edging. When done, you can embellish your handiwork with a quaint blanket stitch trim in a contrasting yarn or in numerous other ways.

Okay, let's get crackin'. Hold the needle with your two cast-on stitches in your left hand and the empty needle in your right hand. As you knit, you will transfer stitches from the left to the right needle. When the left needle is empty, you switch needles so the needle with the stitches is back in your left hand, ready to repeat the process.

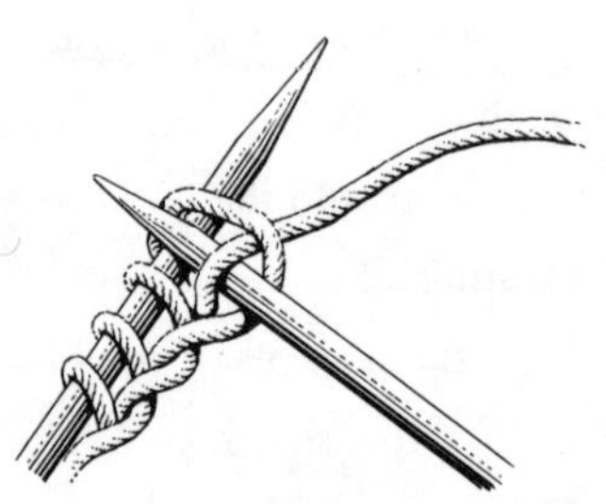

Holding the needles a few inches from the tips, between your thumb and first couple of fingers, and the working yarn in back of the left needle, insert the tip of the right needle into the front of the first stitch, moving it from left to right. With your right index finger, bring the yarn between the needles from back to front and from left to right (see the top illustration above). I know, it's tricky and clumsy right now but *it will* get easier.

Take a deep breath. Pull the right needle with its loop of yarn around the tip toward you and through the stitch, dropping the old stitch off of the left needle (see the bottom illustration on the facing page). You now have a new stitch on the right needle. Tug gently on the working yarn to tighten up the stitch slightly.

Repeat these steps for each stitch to the end of the row. When your left needle is empty, switch needles and start again, moving stitches from the left to right needle.

Yarnovers

This is a variation on a knit stitch, but it allows you to increase your knitting with just an extra wrap of your working yarn. It's one of the more visible methods of increasing the number of stitches per row.

To make a yarnover between two knit stitches, bring the yarn to the front between the two needles. The yarn should be between a knit stitch on the right needle and a knit stitch on the left needle. Bring the yarn up and over the right needle. Now insert the right needle into the stitch on the left needle. Wrap the yarn around the tip of the right needle and pull it through the stitch, slipping the left stitch off the needle, as you would with a plain old knit stitch. You have just created a new stitch and an open space in your knitting.

Randy: wanton or lecherous.
"When Angela felt randy, which always seemed to happen during a quilting bee, she tried to think of her favorite passage in the Old Testament."

The Bind-Off

Funeral, not one's:
not one's business; none of one's concern.
"'It's not your funeral,' Grace told her mother, who wanted to know what she was knitting."

It's hard to imagine but you will reach the end of your project. You need "bind off" to get your new garment off the needles and create a final edge to your work. Here's the easiest way.

Knit two stitches. Now insert the tip of your left needle into the front of the first stitch on the right needle (the one farthest from the tip). Pull it up and over the second stitch and off the needle so only one stitch remains on the right needle. You just bound off one stitch. Knit another stitch and repeat the process, pulling the first stitch over the second, reducing your stitches from two to one each time. Continue across your final row until you only have one stitch remaining. Cut the yarn, leaving about a six-inch tail. Pull it through your last stitch and pull to tighten.

Weave in Ends

When your garment is knitted up, there's still a bit of work to be done. There will be some loose strands here and there. Don't clip these! Instead, thread a yarn end into a tapestry needle (which looks like a big sewing needle and has a big eye), and weave the end in and out of a place that won't be visible, such as the edge or a seam. When the yarn is secure, cut off the remaining yarn.

Join a New Ball of Yarn

When knitting most garments, you'll have to use more than one ball or skein of yarn. Join new balls at the beginning or end of a row, never in the middle. Tie the old yarn and the new yarn together with a loose knot, leaving tails of six inches or more to weave in later. Start knitting with the new working yarn. When you are done with your garment, loosen the knot and weave in each end. Don't worry, they won't unravel.

The Shawl

Now that you have the basics under your belt, let's get started knitting your shawl before the weather turns blustery. You will be starting with two stitches, which will form the point at the

KEEPING COZY

It was *cold* on the frontier. Bone-chilling, limb-numbing, killing cold. Cold that many of us have never felt, at least for any length of time, since the invention of Polartec and central heating.

In addition to sleeping next to each other (and sometimes livestock) to maximize body heat, there were a few other things prairie women used to keep warm. They filled hot-water bottles and warmed their feet with them. They wrapped hot rocks in blankets, and they put glowing coals in bed warmers.

These days, it's not necessary to risk setting your feet on fire to keep cozy. I'm not suggesting outfitting yourself in head-to-toe fleece (too newfangled) or turning up the thermostat (too indulgent). Rather, I like taking the best of the prairie (snuggling up to a warm body, layering quilts) and mixing it with the new (taking a bath, wrapping yourself in a chenille throw, and pulling on down jackets and rain-resistant boots and slickers) if you need to brave the elements. And the biggest improvement for prairie gals is being able to opt for snug pants over drafty skirts and petticoats. That's just good sense.

WHAT YOU WILL NEED

Yarn: 3 skeins Cascade 220 (100% Peruvian highland wool; 220 yards/100 gram), or about 660 yards of a worsted-wool (medium-weight) yarn of your choice in a color of your choice

Size 11 US 32-inch circular needles (you'll knit using these like straight needles— that is, when you finish transferring all your stitches from the left needle to the right, switch hands and start the process over again, always working from left to right needle— but you'll need the piece that connects the two needles to hold your ever-growing garment) or whatever size needles will help you achieve a gauge you like

Tapestry needle

Finished size:
64 inches wide at the top, approximately
48 inches long at the center

Gauge:
3 stitches = 1 inch in garter stitch

bottom of your triangular shawl, and knitting your way up to the top of the shawl, increasing one stitch on every row.

First, you need to knit a swatch if you are using a yarn other than the one I recommend. Cast on 20 stitches and knit until your work is about 4 inches high. Lay a ruler in the middle of your square and carefully measure how wide your swatch is. Divide your 20 stitches by the width. This is your gauge. Hopefully, you are somewhere in the ballpark of three stitches to the inch (your swatch would be almost seven inches wide). If it's close, that's fine for this shawl. When knitting sweaters and garments that require more exact fits, hitting the recommended gauge becomes critical.

Cast on 2 stitches. Row 1: Knit 1, yarnover, knit 1–3 stitches. Row 2: Knit 1, yarnover, knit 2–4 stitches. Row 3: Knit 1, yarnover, knit to end—1 stitch increased. Repeat Row 3 for pattern. Continue knitting until you have 170 stitches on your needles, or until the shawl is 62 inches wide. Bind off.

At this point, you should "block" your shawl, which is a way of stretching and evening out your knitting. Lightly mist it with water, shape it as you desire (pinning it down to a towel or carpet with straight pins if necessary), and dry flat. Weave in the ends with a tapestry needle, and wear with prairie pride.

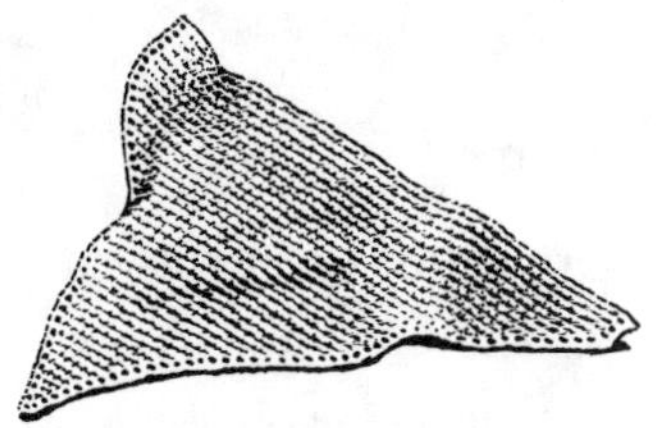

TIP ☞ *Pin a vintage broach or sew buttons onto your shawl (note that anything too heavy can stretch your shawl).*

- *Whipstitch (see p. 87–88) a trim around the edge of the shawl, using a yarn in a contrasting color.*
- *Add fringe to both sides of your shawl.*
- *With a yarn in a contrasting color threaded through a tapestry needle, embroider the outline of a flower, prairie dog, or cherry using a simple backstitch (see p. 76).*

GATHERINGS

QUILTING BEE

I've participated in knitting circles before and love to craft while talking and connecting with other women, but since what little I know about quilting culture and quilting bees comes from watching *How to Make an American Quilt*, I called up my friend and avid quilter Susie Stevenson to get her take on the quilting bee.

Traditionally, women would gather to work on one quilt together, usually a wedding quilt. Since they needed a large, central gathering place, they often met at a church and sang hymns or read the Bible while quilting. They could only meet at certain times of the year because of hard winters, planting season, and harvest time. When they did gather, typically 10 to 12 women would sit around a large wooden frame and work on a project, which might take several bees to complete. In between bees, they often worked on individual blocks and then came together at the quilting bee to assemble the many blocks.

Quilters used whatever they had. They recycled old quilts and clothing, used blankets or raw cotton for batting (the middle layer of the quilt), or just put a fresh top on a worn quilt. They also used the bee to trade fabrics. If they didn't have a frame, women could place chairs in a square, facing toward each other, and stretch the fabric over the seat and pin it to the back of the chairs. When the wedding quilt was completed, women would then work on a group project for different members of the bee.

Today, quilting guilds and bees still gather and enjoy lively conversation and companionship. If you plan on throwing an old-fashioned quilting bee, gather a group of experienced quilters to design and make a group quilt. Spend the first meeting choosing the design and colors. It might make sense to delegate different portions of the quilt to different women so that it can be pieced together in advance and then quilted as a whole with batting and backing over a frame at the bee. As they used to, rotate cooking and babysitting duties. If you're not all religious, consider having women take turns telling stories or reading from a favorite book.

It's much easier to work on individual projects. Supply snacks, beverages, strong lighting, and plenty of needles, thread, and various quilting supplies. Make sure there are comfortable chairs for everyone. Give quilters fabric squares and a thimble as party favors. They'll definitely have a hankering for another quilting bee, even if it *is* harvest time.

Slick: to fix or dress up.

"Belinda got slicked up for the ice cream social, hoping she'd see George."

THE PARLOR

I was born to sit, play, knit, read, and dance (but not sing) in a front parlor. In our ranch house, we only had a big living room, so I made do, as a prairie gal is wont to do. I practiced a slick disco step with my dad on the braided rug. I played games on the floor with my brothers. I tried to learn how to crochet hunkered down on the couch. I watched *The Waltons* in a rocking chair with my grandmother. Our living room was the heart of our home. It was where we gathered and came together.

Not much has changed. When I visit my family or invite people into my home, we spend most of our time in the living room, our modern-day parlor. It's here where I, as a modern-day prairie gal, practice the more genteel pursuits. In a deep armchair, I knit with my makeshift knitting circle. I try to learn the latest dance moves, usually without much success. I curl up on the couch and pen notes to friends and family. I sit down with friends for conversation and a glass of wine. I do my very best to keep my work out of the living room (after all, it's not called the "work room"). Following are a few ways to enrich your experience in the parlor, but think about all the ways you already use this special room for the lighter side of life, be it on the prairie, in town, or even in one of those newfangled neighborhoods called "suburbs." Move the piles of paperwork, the computer, and boxes of tax files into another, more appropriate workspace. This room should be all about *living*.

CREATE CALLING CARDS

During my younger years, I longed for a business card. Neither of my parents had one, as my dad worked in a factory and my mom was a waitress. Handing out crisp cards with my name permanently inscribed on them denoted a step up in the world. For all their oily networking connotations, they also seemed refined and genteel.

Once I had a business card—my first job out of school—I handed them out to friends, family, and the occasional passerby. But it's nice to have cards that are about *you*, not your career. These days, I carry two cards: those I give out when I want to drum up business or make a work contact and those that I give out when I want to remain a bit more mys-

Adventuress:
euphemism for a prostitute or wild woman.
"Once she left her family and headed to the big city, Jane became an adventuress and stopped writing."

terious or present myself as a person first, a wildly successful career gal second.

TIP☞ *Check your printer before running heavy card stock through it; many packages of business card sheets will list the printer requirements.*

WHAT YOU WILL NEED

A computer outfitted with a word-processing program and several script fonts, such as Snell Roundhand or Edwardian Script, and a dingbat font, such as Bodoni Ornaments or Zapf Dingbats

8½-by-11 perforated sheets of 3½-by-5 business cards

Inkjet or laser printer, preferably color

First, decide what information you want to include on your calling card. You could go with the classic—name only—or decide to include a phone number or e-mail address. If you are thinking of putting contact information on your card, remember that you can always write a short note on the back of the card and include a phone number, should you so desire. Including just your name is a lovely way to present yourself, and you won't risk accidentally handing out your phone number to a rowdy or ruffian. Once you give out information, you can't take it back.

TIP☞ *Carry your cards in a sturdy case so they don't get bent or smudged.*

The next thing to do is pick your paper stock. Although you can design and print your cards with a traditional printer or an online company such as VistaPrint®, there's no reason why you, as a prairie gal, can't do it yourself, provided you have the right equipment. Most homesteads these days are outfitted with a computer and a printer. With these two things, you're in business. There are many different sheets of perforated business cards that you can purchase. Avery® has a slew of them. They come in 8½- by-11-inch sheets that run through your printer (just check the requirements on the back of the package). Some even have a border or design on them already. After you print out a sheet of cards, you can carefully pull them apart, tuck them away in your pouch, and hand them out as you see fit.

TIP☞ *For a more rustic look, cut your cards into a different shape (perhaps square) but keep in mind that larger than 3½ by 5 inches will not fit in many business card holders or Rolodexes™.*

Okay, so let's assume you just want your name on your card. For a feminine calling card, I like to feature my full name in a delicate script typeface (i.e., font), such as Edwardian Script ITC or Snell Roundhand. You could also go with a classic block typeface; I fancy Copperplate. Center your name and examine the point size of the type. Fourteen-point type works well for a calling card. Resist the urge to fill up the entire width of the card by enlarging your name. White space is elegant. At this point, I recommend printing out your name on a plain piece of paper. Look at the hard copy to see if you like the typeface and the point size. When you are satisfied, save your document.

Now let's set up your business-card template.

If you are working in one of those newfangled word-processing programs (i.e., Microsoft® Word), you don't need to set margins or copy and paste each card; the software does it for you. Highlight and copy the text of your calling card. Go to the "Tools" menu and select "Labels." Paste your name into the top left box.

TIP *Consider having a rubber stamp made of your name in script. You can then adorn any sort of card stock for a calling card, as well as paper and note cards for personalized stationery.*

Now select "Options." Click on the box to indicate the type of printer you have. Under "Label products," select the type of business card sheets you purchased (for example, "Avery standard"). Now look at the packaging for the business-card sheets and find the product number. Scroll down through the many options until you find a match. Select that line item and click "OK" in the bottom right corner. You'll be returned to the previous window. To finish up, under "Number of labels," select

"Full page of the same label." This ensures you will print an entire sheet of your calling cards. Click "OK" to be taken back to your document.

Your page should now be filled with multiples of your calling card text, spaced out so they match up exactly with your perforated sheets. When you are ready, print out a sheet by feeding it through your printer or putting it in the paper tray (face up or face down, depending on how paper runs through your printer). Carefully separate the cards; trim the edges carefully if the perforation leaves small ridges on the sides.

Hand out your cards judiciously and feel free to pen a small personal note on the back.

TIP ☞ *For a sweet look, add a small piece of electronic clip art or symbol font to your card. For instance, center a small flower or flourish below your name. For my card shown on p. 127, I used 14-point Edwardian Script for my name and added a 12-point Bodoni Ornaments dingbat below it. I like black type but you could easily choose to print your cards with a dark color for the text or art. Lovely, isn't it?*

DISCOVER THE ART OF LETTER WRITING

A woman on the frontier could never have imagined a time when she would be able to communicate instantly with a friend half a world away on a telephone, cellular phone, computer, BlackBerry®, or

Sidekick®. She wrote a letter. She had no choice.

But you *do* have a choice, so once in a while sit down and write a handwritten letter to someone dear. Be it heartfelt or breezy, brief or verbose, a penned note is a gift so simple to offer yet so meaningful (and yes, impressive) to receive. I like to write cards for all occasions but my favorite reason for writing a note is when I have no reason at all. It's that much more special because it wasn't required or expected.

WHAT YOU WILL NEED

Black-ink pen

Gorgeous stationery

Make it special. Put together a small box with letter-writing accoutrements: a lovely pen that glides over the page, stamps, address book, special seals or stickers, and most of all, paper. Be it signature stationery or a varied note card collection, keep stationery on hand that feels great to write on and will be a treat to pull out of a mailbox. And create a proper space, perhaps a cozy overstuffed chair or maybe just the kitchen table after everyone else has long gone to bed.

Now that you are properly outfitted, what do you write and how do you write it? For personal correspondence, there are no hard-and-

PERFECT YOUR PENMANSHIP

For a lovely, flowing handwriting worthy of 19th-century letter writing, the key is to use your arm and shoulder, not your fingers and hand, to move the pen. Not only will your handwriting look cramped, but your hand will feel equally cramped and tight when you use your finger muscles to create letters.

To retrain yourself, adjust how you hold and move your pen. It should be held between the thumb and index finger, with the barrel resting on the middle finger. The remaining fingers should curl under toward your palm. Hold your pen loosely with relatively straight fingers; don't grip it. Anything close to this should work okay. Rest the heel of your hand on the page. Make sure your writing arm is free to move.

Practice writing in large script—in the air or on a chalkboard at first—and do your best not to move your wrist or fingers. Pay attention to your shoulder, arm, and back muscles; they are what should be moving the pen. It feels awkward at first, but it will get easier (I swear), and you will notice a new fluidity to your writing.

If your writing looks messy initially, don't fret or throw in the towel. It's to be expected. If you're bored, instead of doodling, practice repeating loops, slashes, and individual letters, using your arm and shoulder muscles. Getting into the rhythm of these handwriting elements will slowly improve your overall script. As you gain more control and precision, reduce the size of your writing. With your new script, try writing some short notes or cards to friends.

fast rules. Begin your letter with a traditional salutation such as "Dear" or "My Sweet." Anyone will appreciate such a caring greeting.

For the body of the letter, spend a few minutes thinking about the person to whom you are writing and what you'd like to convey to him or her. And since this is a one-way communication, you can be candid. Reveal secrets. Tell a friend how obsessed you are with your cat or how you pine for a boy on a neighboring farm. If you make a mistake, just carefully cross it out. Part of the charm of a hand written letter is the missteps that occur when looking for the *bon mot.*

Increase your chances of a response by taking an interest in your recipient. Ask questions about her life. Ask him for his opinions or advice. Posing questions will ensure that the recipient will feel compelled (not obligated) to reply.

Close the letter with a comment about how much the person means to you and how you look forward to hearing from her. Sign your letter with a signature ending, be it "Sincerely yours," "Yours," "Warmly," or "With much love."

TIP☞ *Penning a letter should always be a joy, not a chore. When it starts to feel like work, put your pen down, have a cup of tea* *(see p. 43)**, and return to the note when you feel refreshed and giving.*

LEARN TO WALTZ

While my early dancing career pretty much consisted of me mastering the Electric Slide in my bedroom, I always loved cutting a rug, even if it was the braided rag rug in the living room. I boogied with

FASHION ON THE RANGE

Fashion on the range sort of seems like an oxymoron, doesn't it? Well, function and durability were extremely important when it came to making dresses. These garments were built to last. But that's not to say they weren't also intended to be pretty or stylish or flattering. Actually, garments were often more flattering than modern-day frocks because they were all custom-made and perfectly fitted to the wearer, who was usually wearing a corset to smooth and define her hourglass figure.

Fashion trends may have taken a while to spread across the prairie, but many got their news, culture, and dress styles from *Godey's Lady's Book,* a Philadelphia periodical that influenced women across America throughout much of the 19th century. Nearly every issue featured a dress pattern with measurements, along with poetry, sheet music, and articles. The issue was expensive, so you can imagine how it must have made the rounds from parlor to sitting room in each town.

Why not take a page out of *Godey's Lady's Book* and invite your favorite gals over for a night of fashion? If you can't sew, all is not lost. Gather a pile of your favorite fashion magazines and thumb through them, looking for styles, colors, and trends you think would complement each other. Or take turns going through each other's closet. Anything that doesn't fit gets sent to the tailor for a more figure-flattering fit. Prairie women know the power of proper, curve-hugging tailoring.

my dad, polka-ed with relatives, and pretended to waltz with Prince Charming. While square and contra dancing were popular pastimes on the prairie, I prefer the genteel *pas de deux* (dance for two) action of a lovely waltz, a dance that became popular in the United States during the nineteenth century.

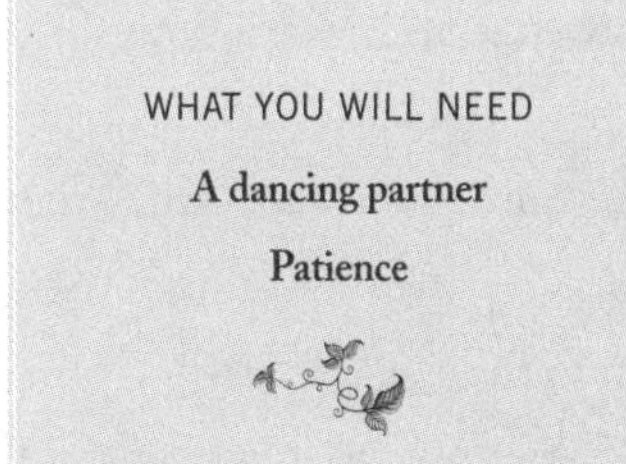

The waltz is a dance in three-quarter time, with a strong emphasis on the first beat. Basically, that means that the beat is *one* two three, *one* two three...The tempo is often slow and the movements of the dancers are long, flowing, and graceful. Because the movements are slow and deliberate, you have the opportunity to be dramatic and expressive.

Waltzing is one of the easiest dances to master, as you can waltz around a room simply by doing four quarter turns of three beats/steps each. These directions are for you; your male partner should do the reverse motion. (If you go back on your left foot, he goes forward on his right. Make sense?)

As the woman, you should have your right hand in your partner's left hand and your left arm resting lightly on the man's right arm with your hand on his shoulder. Start with your feet together.

Begin in "close hold," with the weight on your left foot. Step

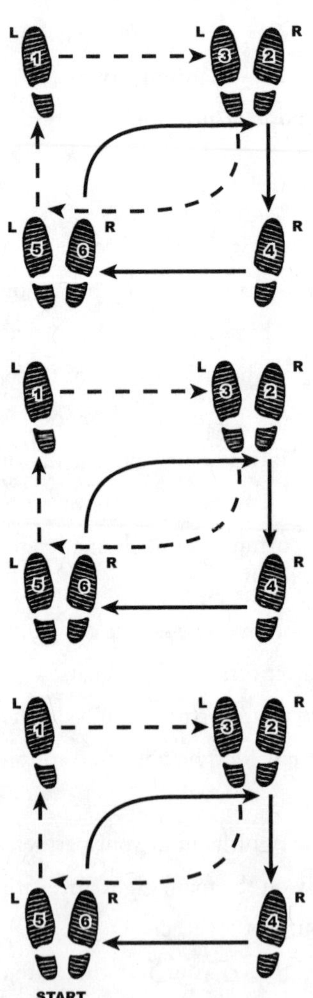

back with your right foot as you count "one." On "two," bring your left foot out to the side. On "three," bring your right foot, tracing an L on the floor, to join your left in closed position.

Now it's all a variation on a theme.

On "one," step back with your left foot. On "two," bring your right foot out to the side. On "three," bring your left foot over to join your right, in a backward L motion, so your feet are together and closed.

On "one," bring the right foot forward. On "two," bring your left foot to the side, and on "three," bring your right foot in a backward L motion to join your left in closed position.

On "one," bring your left foot forward. On "two," bring your right foot to the side, and on "three," bring your left foot, tracing a L on the floor, to join the right in closed position.

You can continue to do this, moving counterclockwise around the room, or you can choose to add more steps.

Tip *Count out loud at first (one two three, one two three) and then silently to yourself as you get the hang of things. Listen to the music, and let that guide your dance as you become more comfortable.*

Dancing should be fun and as long as you are not in a ballroom competition, feel free to add a bit of drama or improvisation. You can do a spin of sorts by breaking close hold while still maintaining contact with your right hand (and his left). Counting *one* two three, *one* two three, slowly dance under your arm hold, moving right and in a clockwise direction. Finish the turn by facing your partner and returning to close hold. Pick up with the basic quarter turn or another step and continue on in your graceful waltz.

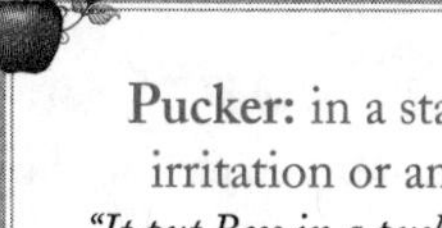

Pucker: in a state of irritation or anger.
"It put Bess in a pucker when Lyman bested her in jacks again and again."

Tip *Follow the lead of your male partner. It may take some getting used to but you'll find it a lovely experience to not always know where you're going but trusting in your partner to care for you.*

LEARN TO PLAY JACKS

I have played my fair share of jacks...and pick-up sticks, tag, hide and seek, marbles, Barbies®, a variety of board games, and anything else that would keep me entertained during long afternoons dodging my brothers. They liked to tease me, so I hid out and played games by myself.

Playing jacks is a great way to develop hand/eye coordination, no matter your age. You can do it by yourself, or with a sibling if you are feeling competitive.

WHAT YOU WILL NEED

Set of jacks
(at least 10 jacks and a small ball)

Flat surface, such as
a sidewalk or a table

With all of the jacks in your hand, shake them and throw them lightly onto a flat surface. If playing on the floor or sidewalk, sit. If you use a table, it's better to stand. Your goal when disbursing the jacks is to get them near each other without having them clumped in one tangled pile.

To play, toss the ball into the air, pick up one jack in the same hand, and catch the ball before it bounces, again doing it with the same hand. Now, repeat the process, this time picking up two jacks. Continue in this manner, picking up one additional jack each time, until you have picked up all the jacks or you fail to gather the correct amount of jacks or catch the ball. When you miss, let the other player(s) take a turn and try to best your score.

TIP *You can also play by bouncing the ball and trying to grab one or several jacks and catch the ball before it bounces a second time. Or you can play by picking up 1 jack 10 times for the first round, 2 jacks 5 times in the second round, 3 jacks 3 times, 4 jacks 2 times, 5 jacks 2 times, and 6, 7, 8, 9, and 10 jacks 1 time.*

THE MODERN PRAIRIE GAL WAY

Back in the day, once a girl passed into womanhood, she usually gave up child's play when she put up her hair. Rather than playing jacks or tag, she spent her time in more useful pursuits, such as cooking and sewing. These days, gals manage to do both. When throwing a cocktail party, why not share your love of all things prairie and all things playful by setting jacks and marbles around the room? You can also leave them in a guest room when you have visitors or keep them in your office desk, pulling them out when you need to relieve a bit of stress.

MIX FURNITURE OIL FOR DUSTING

Can you believe that there was once a time without Endust® and Murphy® Oil Soap? Hard to imagine, I know, but frontier women had to care for their furniture with what they had at hand. So they im-

provised to make their tables, bureaus, bed frames, chairs, and other wooden furniture gleam. Make your home shine with a lovely furniture polish you can whip up in the kitchen.

WHAT YOU WILL NEED

Spray bottle

½ cup olive oil
(you can also use another carrier oil, such as sweet almond or jojoba oil, but they will probably be pricey)

¼ cup lemon juice

Clean cloths

Sterilize a spray bottle (preferably glass) by washing it and then dipping it into a hot-water bath. Dry the bottle. Pour the oil and juice into the spray bottle and gently shake before each use. Spritz your polish onto a clean cloth until it's slightly damp. Use the cloth to polish your furniture, using circular motions. Respray the cloth as needed. Use another cloth to dry the furniture, again polishing in circles. Between use, store in a cool, dark place.

Yields 3/4 cup

SPIN YARN

I've been knitting for years, and I've always been curious about how the wool from a sheep or some other fiber is turned into yarn. During a trip back home, I was treated to a demonstration by Wendy Larson

P

Q

R

S